Software Costing

GW00982873

BCS Practitioner Series

Series editor: Ray Welland

Software Costing

An objective approach to estimating and controlling the cost of computer software

Frank Wellman

Prentice Hall

New York London Toronto Sydney Tokyo Singapore

First published 1992 by
Prentice Hall International (UK) Ltd
Campus 400, Maylands Avenue
Hemel Hempstead
Hertfordshire, HP2 7EZ
A division of
Simon & Schuster International Group

Typeset in 10/12 pt Times
by MHL Typesetting Ltd, Coventry

Printed and bound in Great Britain by
Dotesios Limited, Trowbridge, Wiltshire

Library of Congress Cataloging-in-Publication Data

Wellman, Frank.
   Software costing : an objective approach to estimating and
controlling the cost of computer software / Frank Wellman.
      p.   cm. — (BCS practitioners series)
   Includes bibliographical references.
   IBSN 0-13-818436-4
   1. Computer software—Costs.   I. Title.   II. Series.
QA76.76.C73W45   1992
005.3'0681—dc20   92-5334
                                                          CIP

British Library Cataloguing in Publication Data

A catalogue record for this book is available from
the British Library

ISBN 0-13-818436-4

---

1 2 3 4 5   96 95 94 93 92

To Morag and Iain

Contents

Editorial preface

The aim of the BCS Practitioner Series is to produce books which are relevant for practising computer professionals across the whole spectrum of Information Technology activities. We want to encourage practitioners to share their practical experience of methods and applications with fellow professionals. We also seek to disseminate information in a form which is suitable for the practitioner who often has only limited time to read widely within a new subject area or to assimilate research findings.

The role of the BCS is to provide advice on the suitability of books for the Series, via the Editorial Panel, and to provide a pool of potential authors upon which we can draw. Our objective is that this Series will reinforce the drive within the BCS to increase professional standards in IT. The other partners in this venture, Prentice Hall, provide the publishing expertise and international marketing capabilities of a leading publisher in the computing field.

The response when we set up the Series was extremely encouraging. However, the success of the Series depends on there being practitioners who want to learn as well as those who feel they have something to offer! The Series is under continual development and we are always looking for ideas for new topics and feedback on how to further improve the usefulness of the Series. If you are interested in writing for the Series then please contact us.

This book takes a pragmatic approach to software costing, long recognised as one of the major problem areas in systems development. It is aimed at the practitioner who needs to produce a software cost estimate now. Frank Wellman has extensive practical experience and has distilled this into a good mixture of practical advice, justification and applicable methods for software cost estimation and control.

Ray Welland
Computing Science Department, University of Glasgow

Editorial Panel Members
Frank Bott (UCW, Aberystwyth), John Harrison (BAe Sema), Nic Holt (ICL), Trevor King (Praxis Systems Plc), Tom Lake (GLOSSA), Kathy Spurr (Analysis and Design Consultants), Mario Wolczko (University of Manchester).

Preface

Some time ago I was discussing the preparation of this book with a friend who is a senior executive in a well-known company. His immediate reaction was to suggest that it should be classified as a work of fiction. This, he went on to explain, was a reflection of his own experience in purchasing software where the estimated costs seem to bear no resemblance to the reality of the final bill. This is not an isolated view of software costing and all of us are aware that it has a ring of truth about it. The question that software engineers have to consider seriously is whether they want to continue to be blighted with our past disregard for the commercial aspects of software development. It seems to me, after 30 years in the industry, that we need to address the issue of software costing and make it a high priority in the coming decade, so that general management in all areas of business will feel able to put aside their past scepticism and have some confidence that project estimates will represent much more closely the cost of the installed system. The onus is on all of us within the software industry and I have tried in this book to lay down a practical framework that will contribute to improvement in all aspects of the costing of software.

Many of us, on many occasions, have had that sinking feeling when we face a blank sheet of paper and have to prepare an estimate for a project in a very limited time. There is always the prospect of finding other, past work on which we can base the new system but, all too often, we are confronted by shortcomings in the available information that raise more questions than answers. How does this estimate compare with the actual cost? Why has the cost of bought-in software been omitted? The productivity seems to be unduly optimistic, the project records are incomplete, the person who prepared the estimate has left and there is no explanation of how some figures were prepared. These are just a few of the things we encounter every time we set about preparing an estimate for a new project and this indicates that all too often the foundation on which we are basing those estimates is more than a bit shaky. Despite this, the estimate will be the basis on which the project will be approved and in many instances a contractual commitment for a project will be agreed.

In this book I have not attempted to advance the theory of software costing, but rather to set out a practical basis for day-to-day use that will help all of those involved in costing to improve on the present unsatisfactory position and move rapidly to a situation where the estimate and the installed cost converge. The approach put forward has been used successfully for a number of software projects including new custom developments, modification and re-engineering of existing software and for the costing of packages. It is not a panacea for all the problems we face in the costing of software but, in the absence of any other approach, it provides a foundation for moving forward from the present unsatisfactory situation.

It is unlikely that senior general management in any organisation will read this book from cover to cover. They will, however, derive some benefit from the early chapters and some of the matters discussed later in the text. The book is primarily aimed at those who are involved in software costing, from all standpoints — estimating, project management, QA, auditing and the tendering process. This book is not aimed at students but they should find much of what is said of interest because the practice of software engineering, in the future, will be linked as much to understanding the commercial aspects of software development projects as it will to proficiency in the technical area.

Frank Wellman
Aberdeen 1992

Introduction ·

Software development continues to be a labour-intensive activity using, in the main, highly qualified and expensive people. Over the last decade much more rigorous methods of system design have been developed and adopted across the industry. This has had an important influence on the training of software engineers and has been one of the factors that has focused attention on the need for a more systematic approach to all aspects of software development. However, there still remains a major gap in the software industry — a sound basis for commercial decisions coupled with a consistent and rigorous approach to the costing of software.

We need to look at the cost of a software project in a number of ways: initially, from the general management viewpoint of an investment in a facility that will yield a return to the business; then viewed from the estimating standpoint to establish in detail what is involved and what costs will be incurred — this must be done in close consultation with the designer of the software and the planning of the development as a project. Once an estimate is completed the matter must be referred back to general management to approve the basis of the proposed project and sanction the estimate as the project budget. When a viable project has been agreed then the project manager assumes responsibility for carrying out the development within the agreed budget and timescale. This includes exercising all appropriate cost control procedures and carrying out any agreed amendments to the budget and schedule. Finally there is the retrospective analysis of actual costs to provide the input to future estimating activities.

If we are to become effective in controlling software costs these activities must be recognised and accepted as essential, not optional, and they must be carried out in a coherent way. That will require a change of attitude and practice and the recognition that estimating and cost control are important skills on which the success of the project depends — just as important as skill in design and program development. Astounding technical advances in hardware and brilliant young people designing and implementing systems are the hallmark of our industry — and long may it remain so — but these alone will not sustain the IT industry nor establish software engineering as a mature profession that can provide systems for all facets of our work and leisure.

Since the first flight of a very simple aircraft in 1903 we have come to rely on air transport for defence, business and pleasure in a way never imagined at the outset. The aerospace industry has become established, in a relatively short timescale, as a major force in design, construction and operation, embracing many branches of engineering as well as other disciplines. The IT industry is running a somewhat similar course and from some relatively simple software applications in the early days it has become a powerful influence on all aspects of our daily life in a period of about 40 years.

Over that time progress in software has largely been focused on the technical aspects at the expense of attention to the provision of a framework for consistent quality. In the past there was scant attention paid to standards and establishing good procedures and practices but that is now being addressed and during the early 1990s the situation will improve with the publication of many important standards both in Europe and the USA. We must also learn from other branches of engineering, particularly the commercial aspects, such as costing, as these will be a vital element in ensuring a viable and stable future for the industry. Most branches of engineering have well-established estimating procedures and have engineers committed to the estimating process. The software industry has no such facilities and as part of the process of establishing software engineering as a mature profession it is important to focus on these hitherto neglected aspects. The American Association of Cost Engineers defines cost engineering as 'that area of engineering practise where engineering judgement and experience is utilized in the application of scientific principles and techniques to problems of cost estimation'. These principles and techniques include business planning, profitability analysis, cost estimating, cost control, project management, planning and scheduling.

Few software engineers whose daily work involves system development projects have a satisfactory grounding in cost engineering, as defined by the AACE, and indeed estimating, project management and cost control seem to be areas of particular weakness. Software cost engineering needs, therefore, to be seen as an important area of skill and much more encouragement needs to be given to people to take up the challenge of software cost management.

This book addresses the many issues involved in software costing and emphasises its importance from the initial assessment of the proposed investment, through the development process, to paying the bill at the end of the warranty period. An objective and consistent approach is proposed in which account is taken of all the items that influence or contribute to the end cost of software. The various chapters address these issues and show how the process of estimating progresses from the macro stage into more detail and then feeds into the design and planning of the project. This continues through into cost control, fiscal audit and ultimately on to project review and completion of the cycle by post-project review and the provision of additional data for future estimating activities.

Those who commission software, the customer, and those who carry out the development, the contractor, have a responsibility to ensure that software costing is fully effective and that all those involved strive continually to improve the process. Many of the problems and shortcomings that arise today are due as much to the omission of major elements of cost at the very beginning and to a misunderstanding between the customer and the contractor, as they are to shortcomings in the models and methods of estimating. Better software costing will come from focusing on all of the issues involved and identifying the ways in which these can be improved.

The book is aimed at software engineers involved in the procurement and development of software — those who buy packages, those who commission custom software, those who prepare project plans and estimates, and those who manage software development. The approach set out in this book will provide them with a more rigorous approach and make a contribution to the introduction of more professional cost management procedures in software engineering.

1 Justification for software development

1.1 Recognising that costs must be justified

The IT industry is still a young industry that has not fully found its roll in support of the operational and functional activities in industry, commerce and government that depend on information. There have been many applications of IT that have made a significant contribution to different aspects of our lives — more effective control of the fiscal aspects of business, more effective control of process systems in industry, improved safety and security, convenience of improved services to the public and advances in leisure services, but in an overall sense these are scratching at the surface. To a certain extent the way in which IT applications have developed in the past has been influenced by a lack of understanding of the value of information by senior management across all of these sectors. In the past decisions had to be made and management could not always wait for up-to-date information before action was initiated. These habits die hard and have not been helped by unsatisfactory management information systems and poor quality databases. It is only now that we are beginning to awaken to the realisation that in order to get the best from IT it is necessary to assess the facilities available, harness the available skills and examine how these can be used to produce quality systems that will be of most value to business and mankind in general. This is perhaps best manifest in the realisation that information is of strategic importance and many large organisations are now becoming much more aware of the need to identify what they see as their strategic information systems (SIS). Similarly at the operational level information is vital to day-to-day functions and underpins effective decision making which in turn has led to the identification and development of decision support systems (DSS). This is not yet a uniform view even within any particular sector of the economy, let alone across all sectors. There are still a lot of people to be converted to the view that IT has a positive role and tangible value in all areas of human endeavour.

Perhaps the greatest weakness, however, in the growth in application of IT is that there is still a significant body of people who question the need for justifying expenditure in terms of an identified return over a specific period of time.

Major projects such as Concorde, the exploration of space and indeed much pioneering medical work on human embryos and organ transplants could not be justified on a strict financial assessment and are justified as having national benefit or value to mankind. However, there are very few projects, whether IT or in other spheres, that can be classified in this way or even called 'developmental', or just done as research to find out something new. These research activities should be set apart from the majority of projects and the financing of such work dealt with on an individual financial justification basis. But even where a project is identified as research or development it must be fully costed and project management and control procedures applied throughout. All other IT developments should be treated as an investment which must have an identified objective and an expected financial return, based on an assessment of the level of financial risk involved. Indeed in most cases the risk will be very low and the return substantial. However, this is only the case if a thorough and objective assessment is made and steps taken from the outset to ensure that the benefits can be achieved — vague expectations are not an acceptable alternative to a determination to reap the benefits. This matter is discussed further in Section 1.7 of this chapter when the idea of a post-implementation benefit audit is introduced, and again referred to as part of life cycle costing in Chapter 10.

The next decade should be very exciting and rewarding for all those engaged in the IT industry but if we are to make the most of that opportunity it is essential that we develop the necessary business skills to be able to assess where, when, and how IT can yield substantial tangible benefits. Of particular importance in this context is software. Over the last three decades much of the development effort and investment of the IT industry has been directed at the design of hardware, making use of new materials and techniques, that has resulted in enormous increases in processing power at prices that are a fraction of those even 10 years ago. At the same time, although there have been some advances in the techniques and tools available for software development, software has continued to be developed by manpower-intensive means and there has been only a modest gain in overall productivity. Indeed many of the technical advances in software productivity have been neutralised by the ever rising salary scales of software engineers. As a proportion of the total system set-up cost, the cost of software is a major factor. Moreover, when full account is taken of support costs over the life cycle of the system, software accounts for about 90% of the total costs to the end user for running the system. On this basis alone spending on software needs to be examined very closely and the costs justified in terms of benefit.

1.2   IT as a facilitator of business change

Doubt is often cast on the benefit derived from IT systems, particularly the software, because senior management have an impression that software is not robust, is constantly requiring modification and support, and involves more and more investment with very little in the way of recognisable benefit. There is some justification for this point of view, which arises in many cases because there is insufficient attention given, at the outset, to a thorough evaluation of the benefits that will be gained from the use of the system. Many people, even today, do not consider the evaluation of software systems as important and have a quick and superficial look at feasibility, then go straight into a specification and on with what they see as the *real* objective — developing software. The shortcomings should be obvious — cost benefit has been ignored and there is therefore no benchmark against which to judge the acceptability of the system, let alone the validity of the investment. It is not surprising therefore that senior management are often apprehensive about sanctioning spending on new systems. Moreover, they see IT as an administrative overhead that contributes little to the profitability of the organisation. As a consequence, when there are economic pressures and a need for corporate cutbacks, IT is fair game for first-line cuts in spending. This of course does not imply that IT departments should not bear a share of trimming and slimming from time to time. However, the overall place of software in the business environment must now be seen in the context of an essential corporate facility, particularly if there is top-level commitment to the support of strategic information and the use of decision support systems. It follows that the IT department should be regarded as having an essential corporate support role.

Far too many people in the IT industry, and on the periphery, are intoxicated with the high-technology aspects of software and regard it as some form of exclusive commodity that should attract ever increasing investment without any proper initial justification or an expectation of a satisfactory return in a realistic timescale. Another contributory factor to the poor image of software as a corporate asset is that in many instances, even where satisfactory pre-project evaluation has been carried out, little or no attention is given to ensuring that the system, once installed, is used in a way that will yield the expected benefits. Software is the principal means by which the power of IT is brought to effective use in the many and varied ways in which it impinges on our business and social life, and we must focus much more attention on ensuring that that power is fully utilised by end users and that the software application system yields the planned benefit.

Another shortcoming is that IT has far too often in the past been used to automate, or just *put wheels under*, existing manual practices with often only minor and doubtful benefit. The primary objective for the future must be to examine how IT can make a full contribution to the efficiency and effectiveness of working practices. If software is to be of any real value to an organisation then certain points must be recognised, from the conceptual stage of every project, as follows:

- Savings in minor administrative areas such as paper, forms, etc. are likely to be of no consequence and only detract attention from the real value of a system. Indeed minor savings which are unlikely to be visible in practice, if promoted as benefits, are the sorts of thing that are likely to influence senior management adversely when asked to sanction a proposed development, particularly at times of fiscal constraint. It must be said, however, that some very successful projects have been based on major economies in administration.
- Cost saving, not cost cutting, is the important factor. Cost cutting is totally misleading in terms of introducing IT systems — it is concerned with short-term survival and has no relevance to assessing how the power of new IT systems can be of most value in the corporate environment. Software in particular can contribute to changes in business practices and provide a

foundation for improvements in competitive and profitable trading, but as a general rule not as a short-term solution.

- IT is a facilitator of change in business practice and needs to be considered in this context before any system development is undertaken, be it a new development or a major enhancement to operational systems. The flexibility of software provides the basis for doing things in a different way — often involving radical changes — that could not be considered by manpower-intensive means alone. It is the combination of manpower skills and software facilities that makes many new business practices possible. In this context it must be borne in mind from the outset that system design and development is *not* about saving money — it may be one facet and it may be relevant in some instances — but far too much emphasis has been placed on this negative aspect to the neglect of other, often more valuable, positive aspects.
- The areas on which attention should be focused are those where IT can facilitate and support one of the following:

  · a new service or product;
  · an increase in productivity;
  · a decrease in production costs;
  · an increase in market share;
  · an increase in turnover and profit;
  · an increase in safety;
  · protection of the environment;
  · improvement of the working environment.

These are aspects of the business that are often not fully considered in the context of IT and to achieve substantial benefit in any of these areas an increase in investment in software will often be necessary. The potential benefits should be significant and justify the risk and the commitment to change if the project is to be considered seriously. It is important therefore that specific objectives are identified and quantified at the outset. 'An increase in productivity' is a worthy aim but it must be made much more specific and identify the following:

- Whether it is applicable to one, some or all products.
- What level of increase is being targeted.
- What the potential market value is and what steps have to be taken to sell the increased volume.

It is implicit from this that any situation where IT is to be considered as an enabling facility will involve expertise right across the organisation and may well incur significant costs outside the area of IT, such as additional raw materials and sales effort, and these must be taken fully into account in the overall appraisal. Despite its importance there is no established and accepted basis for justification assessment and this is just one of the problems that face anyone attempting to carry out a formal evaluation. One consequence is that many organisations sidestep the issue. A study of IT use in UK building societies, carried out in 1989 (Thresher (1)), indicates quite clearly that attention to justification is somewhat scant even when the investment is of a substantial nature. The report quotes one manager as saying 'In large projects we mostly go by gut feel. If the project is small we try for a return-on-investment basis.' Another manager indicated that if the project was of a strategic nature it was done without any formal justification but if it was efficiency related the project was cost justified. It is evident from this that a lot still needs to be done in the area of strategic evaluation of IT systems. Software engineers must accept therefore that from here on they will need to function as part of the business team and use their skills to achieve specific corporate goals rather than sit on the sidelines offering expensive solutions to poorly defined requirements. A much more positive and assertive stance must be taken by the software industry, as a whole, so that the enormous advantages to be gained from more effective harnessing of the immense power of well-targeted and well-constructed systems can be realised.

1.3 Supporting systems by a sound information system strategy

It is essential to support operational systems by an effective overall information system (IS) strategy on an ongoing basis because, although it is possible to gain competitive advantage from IT, it is not sustainable unless the supporting IT policy itself continues to be fully effective. It is necessary therefore to look periodically at the IT systems and services themselves, outside of the framework of a particular software system or application area. However, the strategy should not dominate the application because the justification for any IT investment only comes from the value of using the systems in the corporate environment. The results of surveys on the use of IT are usually presented showing spend as a proportion of turnover. Companies will look at this kind of data and assume that, because their own spending on IT is close to the 'norm' for the relevant economic sector, their IT activities must be satisfactory. The other misleading aspect of such figures is that the whole IT budget is usually only a small percentage of turnover $(2-3\%)$ and does not therefore justify much attention in relation to other aspects of the business incurring much higher costs. IT derives its benefit from the value added to the business effectiveness, such as improving operational efficiency and supporting business expansion. The level of investment in IT and the attention it warrants should therefore be dictated by the benefit gained from the use of the systems. The issues that really need to be considered are as follows:

- Have the systems in use been evaluated on the basis of a business investment?
- Is the full benefit (financial return) being gained from the systems already in operation?
- Are there other software applications that should be implemented that will increase the overall effectiveness of the business, such as increased competitive advantage?

These are the key issues when carrying out an IS strategy study and only when these matters have been addressed is it possible to decide whether the present investment in IT systems is satisfactory.

Often IT departments grow in a piecemeal way — recruiting more staff because of more work, installing more hardware to meet a growth in demand from users. There is a need, periodically, to carry out an IS strategy review directed at the IT operational environment — it is a matter of auditing the technical support environment which provides the means of delivering the power of IT to end users. The IS strategy review should focus on the following:

- Volume and mix of the IT activities.
- Spread throughout the organisation.
- Geographic distribution of services and user locations.
- Priority in terms of business dependence.
- Demand level — daily, weekly, monthly.
- Security, safety, recovery and backup arrangements.
- Overall business risk and exposure through IT.

The objective is to ensure that the IT *support environment* is fully cost effective and can provide end users in the business with the facilities necessary to *use* the relevant software to exploit the competitive business edge. This requires careful judgement to ensure that a proper balance is sustained between a lean and mean service and one that is overprovided.

1.4   A Sound business evaluation

At the beginning of any proposed development there must be an examination of the particular area of business or business practice with the aim of establishing the following:

- How is it done at the moment?
- How could IT be used to change this practice or contribute more?
- What will be involved in terms of changes in business practice and in terms of IT?
- How can the changes be undertaken?
- What is the risk?
- What is the cost?
- What will be the benefit?
- Over what timescale should the changes be introduced?
- Over what timescale will the cost be incurred?
- Over what timescale will the benefits be achieved?

Any development in a business environment is a trade-off between requirements, cost and benefit. It may not always be prudent to undertake the whole system development in one step — a phased approach should be examined as it may be more attractive to proceed with the whole development if part of the investment focused in the core of the system can yield a return before follow-on phases are commissioned in which other user facilities are developed. This is one of the ways in which investment risk can be minimised.

One of the major considerations in making an investment in any area of a business is the risk involved. The following are some aspects of risk related directly to software that should to be taken into account.

Software performance

If the proposed system is innovative in any sense there is always a risk that it may not achieve the expected performance, or in the extreme not function and have to be abandoned.

Late delivery

This may occur even in situations where no innovation is involved and a system that is not commissioned is not functioning to generate a return on the investment. A sensitive market opportunity, that is time dependent, may be lost or the expected benefit greatly diminished due to late delivery of a support system.

Third-party software

Where a package is being bought in, either to meet the application requirements or to support it, there is a potential risk of late delivery or under performance.

Corporate data security

Every time an organisation commits itself to greater, or wider, use of IT there is increased exposure to the misuse of corporate data through fraud, industrial espionage or corruption by viruses.

Market opportunity

Markets are always volatile and the basis of any assessment, based on a window of opportunity or niche, can change without prior warning. This includes situations where there is a planned investment in IT as a platform for a business activity such as expanding a service or introducing a new product. As mentioned earlier, these are situations where IT is being used to gain a competitive edge. The volatile market opportunity also applies within the IT industry in situations where a new or improved package is being developed to sell into a potential market.

Every business decision is a matter of balancing the risk against the potential benefit. Software development projects must be seen in that context because they will be judged in that way by senior management. The software engineers' role is to contribute to the following:

- Thinking out every aspect of the project.
- Thinking out the value of success or consequences of failure.
- Assessing the probability of success or failure.
- Identifying the weak areas.
- Quantifying the costs involved in getting the system operational.
- Quantifying the benefits from using the system.
- Presenting this assessment to management as a business appraisal.

1.5   Business benefit

The potential value of a software system is no more self-evident than is the cost of the system — benefit has to be identified and quantified and the timescale for the return on the investment must be estimated. The benefits will usually be a mixture of direct, indirect, tangible and intangible and should always be identified as such.

Direct savings

These will come from the business area and from the IT area when it is a replacement system. The main areas of saving are likely to be the following:

- Manpower.
- Equipment.
- Supplies.
- IT services (equipment, supplies and even manpower).

Increased operational control

This will be an indirect benefit because it is always a moot point as to how much is *gained* from the use of information. The potential benefits from increased control of data are as follows:

- Improved data accuracy and availability.
- More effective use of information at all levels.
- Improved decision making.
- Improved response times.
- Improved customer services.

However, whether these have any real value in practice depends on the extent to which the available information is used internally and externally in the conduct of the business. It is well known to all those who have carried out consultancy or systems studies that a lot of decision making, at all levels, is based on informal practices and informal sources of information.

Business expansion

This area is potentially the most beneficial as it will yield the biggest returns on the IT investment, assuming of course that the development was planned as a facilitator of business change and qualified in terms of increased turnover and profit. The potential benefits will come from the following:

* Introduction of a new service or product.
* Expansion into a new geographic area.
* Targeting a larger share of the market.
* Exploiting a competitive edge.

Corporate effects

In some situations there may be a value from IT that is not attributable to a specific part of the business, such as production, finance, marketing, but nevertheless yields a tangible benefit such as the following:

* Improved cash flow.
* Doing more for less cost.

Such overall improvements in efficiency should be taken into account providing they can be attained in practice and are significant and can be measured as a 'before' and 'after' change. Much more important, however, is the corporate control of information. What is now abundantly clear is the level of *loss* from failure to take care of corporate data. Over 40% of organisations that fail to get control of corporate information go out of business within a year. What is not fully understood by many people is that insolvency is not an event — it is an operational state of an organisation arising from a failure to gather and use information in a timely manner.

1.6   Other factors in justifying software

Apart from the intangible benefits that may come from installing new or improved software, change may be forced on organisations from outside in a number of ways and in some cases there is no choice but to respond immediately. This involves making an investment that has no measurable benefit. One example is a statutory requirement which involves the control of information or preparation of periodic reports. Examples are data protection legislation, value-added tax and oil and gas production reporting. Although there is no direct benefit there is often a direct fiscal penalty for non-compliance and that can certainly be quantified. Avoidance of such penalties by compliance can be considered as an incentive and the penalties themselves regarded as a 'saving'.

Another area which may well justify investment is change in the market place, such as having no choice but to respond to challenges — there is always the danger of losing market share or having to catch up if a response is delayed significantly.

This situation applies across all areas of the economy — including defence — and IT has to be considered as one of the resources available in responding to the challenge of change.

We are all aware of the misuse of data and the need for the protection of data and software from various sources such as the following:

- Criminal fraud.
- Unauthorised access to data (hacking).
- Accidental and deliberate corruption of data.
- Software viruses.

Countermeasures, whether they be improved security systems or virus detectors, cost money and have to be assessed in terms of risk and potential loss. The whole matter of software protection and 'insurance' must be taken fully into account when planning and costing software.

Finally it is important to mention the most intangible factor of all, namely quality of service both internal and external — what price, what value? Those organisations who practice total quality management (TQM) will accept that quality cannot be quantified but its value is incalculable.

1.7   Quantifying cost and benefit

It will be seen in later chapters that it is not sufficient to state a total cost or the benefit expressed in some simple form such as 'payback period'. The benefit needs to be considered in the context of an investment. The information needed to make a proper assessment is as follows:

- Total cost.
- Cost profile.
- Rate of return.
- Payback period.
- Ongoing benefit (contribution to profit).
- Maximum negative cash flow.

The finer detail will depend on practices within the particular organisation and may include the following:

- Opportunity cost, which is an assessment of other ways of using the money for corporate benefit. In its simplest form it amounts to the addition of interest over the development period, at a rate that would be derived from simply putting the money in the bank, or the interest incurred directly if the money has to be borrowed for the project. Opportunity costs are usually considered on a wider basis taking account of the overall benefit and risk in relation to other competing corporate investment needs.
- A discounted cash flow (DCF), particularly if the investment and return are over a number of years. DCF seems periodically to go out of fashion, particularly in periods when interest rates and inflation are volatile, but it is

a useful way of producing a single figure — net present value (NPV) — which is an effective way of comparing the cost of different options over a given period.

The credibility of project estimating in the software industry is fairly low — budgets and timescales are exceeded far too often and to such a large degree that there is always a significant question mark over the attainment of benefit. It is always refreshing to find cases where project budgets are achieved, but even in these cases there is often little evidence that a rigorous financial benefit assessment was made and a cost—benefit carried out, so that the net value of the system cannot be assessed. Taking a wide perspective of experience and published information one can conclude that only about 15% of projects are completed within target of the original budget — that is, with no more than 10% overrun. The following breakdown shows that the majority exceed budget by a wide margin:

- 5% meet initial budget;
- 10% exceed initial budget by 10%;
- 20% exceed initial budget by 25%;
- 30% exceed initial budget by 50%;
- 35% exceed initial budget by at least 100%:

According to DeMarco (3), pre 1981 there were as many as 15% of software projects that produced nothing useful at the end. There are also figures available to indicate that at least 10% of projects exceed the initial budget by several hundred per cent.

It is important therefore to look at benefits in the context of realistic attainment. A good rule of thumb is that potential benefits should be at least five *times* costs. This is on the basis of a pessimistic view of attaining the benefit and a pessimistic view of bringing the project in on budget. If the budget goes up significantly and all the benefits are not realised then with a five times margin there is a possibility that the outcome will be at least breakeven.

Another good rule of thumb in assessing justification is to set the following targets:

- For high-risk projects the payback period should be short — 2 years from going operational — and the benefit—cost ratio should be at least 5:1 and achievable within 4 years.
- For low-risk projects the payback period should be no more than 3 years and the full benefit achievable within 5 years.

Experience shows that these are easily attainable goals; indeed, in a significant number of projects it has been possible to target and achieve returns as high as 10 times the investment in software within a 5 year period. However, benefits do not happen just as a consequence of installing a system — *benefits have to be worked for* and two reasons why systems fail to achieve the original expectations are the following:

1. A shortfall in training, resulting in a failure to make effective use of the facilities available in the system.

2. No monitoring of how the system is being used in the operational environment, resulting in a failure to tune the system to ensure that it is yielding the most value.

It is incumbent on senior management not only to ensure that the investment in software systems is justified when the budget is approved but also to take steps to ensure that those benefits are achieved in practice. There is a very strong case for introducing a scheme of post-implementation benefit audit that is conducted periodically after a system goes live to establish how the system is functioning specifically in terms of the expected benefits. Such an audit should aim to quantify the benefits on a time base from implementation. Indeed, carrying out a post-implementation benefit audit should become standard practice in all organisations and be conducted either by the QA department or as a joint activity between the users, the IT department and the appropriate fiscal control group.

2 System feasibility and macro estimating

2.1 Quantifying feasibility and benefit

On whatever basis the software development is thought to be justified, and it may often be a mixture of both operational cost saving and business expansion, there must be a formal justification prepared as discussed in the preceding chapter. This must be followed up by an assessment of technical feasibility and a more detailed macro investment profile covering not only the total cost involved but also the timescale of that spending and the appropriate timescale over which the resulting financial benefit will be achieved. It is, however, important to understand clearly what is involved in estimating and the impact that good estimating can have on all aspects of a project. Equally it should be clearly understood by all concerned, whether senior management or young technicians, that the rapid pulling of numbers out of the air relating to time or money will inevitably result in erroneous costs and timescales, and if any decision is made on this basis it may result in the following:

- Serious exposure due to gross underestimating.
- A potentially serious waste of resources if it involves ill-conceived technical innovation.
- A missed opportunity if the quick estimate of costs is thought to be too high compared with the perceived benefits and no action is taken.

DeMarco (3) has placed considerable emphasis on understanding quantification and defines a metric as a measurable indication of some qualitative aspect of a system. In the case of software systems the quantitative aspects are as follows:

- Scope.
- Size.
- Complexity.
- Cost.
- Elapsed time.

These quantitative aspects relate to the following:

- The software system.
- The construction project.

It is essential that aspects such as scope and size are quantified by specification and that complexity is known and understood by the examination of feasibility and the identification of a low-risk approach to development and implementation.

Technical feasibility studies are not widely practised in situations where the software development is seen as 'straightforward' and do not involve any innovation, nor where the software module is an addition to an existing system. However, consideration of technical feasibility should become a routine part of the pre-approval process for the following reasons:

- Design should be examined in the context of construction as well as the context of functionality. There are many instances where software has been designed to meet the functional specification but the design has caused untold problems in development and implementation. This is often due to insufficient understanding of what can be done in practice and insufficient understanding of the development environment.
- Design of a new system should be examined not only from the standpoint of construction but also from that of maintainability.
- Design of modifications should be reviewed from the standpoint of their effect on the integrity of the existing operational system. It is important to establish at an early stage that the new development will function satisfactorily in the existing operational environment and will not adversely affect the performance of other software with which it is required to interact.
- Technical complexity should be established at the feasibility stage. Failure to establish the *true* complexity of a system results in an underestimation of the effort needed for design and development and is a major contributor to project overruns.

Where leading-edge IT is to be used or competitive advantage is sought through the use of IT there is often a need to combine rigorous financial assessment with the assessment of the suitability of new technology. These arguments are not, as some believe, mutually exclusive — the most effective way is to make use of prototyping and piloting to ensure that the system will be viable. This must be done as a positive step in the process of establishing the feasibility and prototyping must be planned and costed as a preliminary investment. This will help ensure that the main development will be successful so that the expected benefits can be realised. In many instances the work done in prototyping can be used directly for specification and design, so it is a matter of investing more in the early stages of software development and gaining the benefit at a later stage.

2.2   Technical feasibility

Embarking on any new development, particularly where it necessitates using new techniques or new technology, involves a certain risk. Over enthusiasm for new technology, often oversold or promoted in the wrong context, can prove to be very misguided and an expensive and even disastrous course to take. Small (2), commenting on a survey of high-technology applications in manufacturing industry, points to the lamentable failure of computer-integrated manufacture

(CIM) and CAD/CAM in the 1980s. In the cases looked at, about 75% of all high-tech investment and about 65% of all medium-technology projects were considered to be at best marginally successful and in far too many instances a failure. Small points to superficial decision making as a significant contributory factor stemming from the lack of an overall strategy, which resulted in piecemeal applications. One consequence of these failures, and wasted investment, is that some companies have taken the view that they do not need new technology to be competitive.

Under enthusiasm — the ultra-conservative 'we only use proven technology' — can also be unsatisfactory as the opportunity to embrace significant potential benefits can be missed. A balanced approach, taking some risk, is more realistic, but the nature of the risk and its influence on the project as a whole must be assessed. The nature and level of risk can be attributed to a number of sources, as follows.

Experience and skill

By involving a team with limited or no experience in the planning of a new system, using a new technique or a new development tool, the most likely consequence will be that the project may well fall far short of expectations, take more effort and cost more to complete over an extended timescale. It is doubtful in such circumstances that the return on the investment will be achieved and the technology is likely to be identified as the cause. It is crucial in such circumstances to learn as much as possible from other organisations who have travelled the same path and also to invest in training in the relevant techniques and technology at the outset.

Unproven technology

Using a technique or facility which has not been proven in application or is a technology transfer from another unrelated application would only be justified if the expected operational benefits from success were significant and if everyone was aware of the high risk from the outset. The project must be seen in the context of leading edge and in such circumstances there must be an alternative technical option with a contingency plan and cost estimate to cover that fallback situation.

The feasibility of any technical design and the examination of complexity can of course be assessed more readily today by using prototyping and developing pilot systems, but again there must be a clear understanding that such work will only produce a model or partial solution for assessment and some measure of risk will still remain in moving to the full system. Any investigative work done on technical feasibility will involve manpower effort and other resources and it is necessary for an estimate to be prepared and approved for this initial work. The objective in prototyping is to examine feasibility and if subsequently the proposal is not seen to be viable then the initial investment, although small, may have to be written off. On the other hand, if the development is subsequently considered viable the risk will have been reduced and some design and development ideas may well have been established.

The aim of the technical feasibility study is not only to define whether it can be done but also to identify much more precisely in business terms the value of success and the cost of failure from the standpoint of the techniques proposed.

2.3   Prototyping and piloting

It is important to draw a clear distinction between prototyping and piloting. Prototyping involves the development of key features of the system as a model to test out techniques. Piloting is the use of a basic features version in a limited but realistic operational environment. In some circumstances a prototype of the system may be used as a limited pilot version to gain further information for input to the design and estimating process. Both uses of prototyping have an important role in the process of establishing a better understanding of how a proposed system will function and work effectively in the target operational environment.

'Experimental' prototyping is likely to cover the following:

• Assessment modelling.
• Evaluation of algorithms.
• Design technique validation.
• Design of test facilities.

Experimental prototyping is a way of representing the methods and solutions that meet the functional requirements and can assist in the reduction of technical risk.

'Exploratory' prototyping usually involves the following:

• Functional representation, particularly of interaction in a multi-user environment.
• Simple working model of the system that may be used as a pilot.
• Representation of user interfacing to maximise effectiveness in the operational environment.
• Evaluation of system modifications and additions to examine the impact on the existing system.

Exploratory prototyping represents the system and the operational environment and is a valuable tool for looking at systems integration aspects and can help in the reduction of application risk.

2.4   Evolutionary development

Faced with a situation where a system may be leading edge or in other ways high risk, it is sensible to consider an approach that will result in a 'satisfactory' outcome to a particular system requirement. In this case 'satisfactory' means a compromise between unacceptable risk and achieving significant benefit from a new application even if the original objective is not fully achievable. Gilb (4) proposed the evolutionary delivery, defined as 'evolutionary because it is based on the principle of a single step forward — feedback — adapt and proceed — feedback — adapt and proceed — feedback — and so on'. This is a recognition of the simple principle that deviations from plan will occur in specification and timing and it is sensible to take limited steps targeted at an initial objective and then adapt to a revised objective. The revised objective may be a higher horizon and not necessarily always falling short of target.

Gilb advocates that 'by conscious and full exploitation of evolutionary ideas, we can not only exercise far better control over risk elements, but we can gain many other important benefits as software engineering managers'. It is better to do this consciously than to start on a project ignoring that risk and then changing tack when a problem is met and pretending that it is possible to 'manage' one's way out of the difficulty.

The process of assessment — justification, feasibility and macro estimating — is not something that should be done 'up front' as activities that are unconnected with the main body of the project before moving on to the system definition and development. In some instances it may be necessary to undertake some outline design work before a decision can be made regarding the viability of the approach. Some organisations are now seeing the value of commissioning a requirement definition and then reviewing this before proceeding with design and development. It would be of immense value if each of these stages were seen in the light of Gilb's evolutionary delivery principle as illustrated in Figure 2.1.

2.5　Design concepts and cost-effective approaches to software

Far too much of software design effort is still focused on individual applications and short-term needs. If the software industry is to advance from this piecemeal, very high-cost, situation then much more attention should be focused on modular design. This must be done as early as possible in the project, even at the feasibility stage, so that parts of the system of a general nature can be identified and considered as possible standard modules. Initially these will be 'outgoing' to build up a components library, but within a short timescale it should be possible to draw from such a source for new developments. If each software development contributed at least one component to a library it would be possible, say within a 2 year period, to have some proven, reusable software with the attendant attraction of much lower cost. Work within specialist organisations such as Raytheon (Lanegran and Grasso (30)) and Toshiba (Matsumoto (31)) over the last decade has shown that the building of software component libraries has a very significant impact on the cost of software, and the level of saving is sufficient now to consider this concept on a much wider basis.

Another important, and related, area is improvement in software development productivity. This is quite distinct from the 'productivity' in terms of rate of code production of individual software engineers discussed in Section 6.5. Boehm and

Figure 2.1
Evolutionary
development and
review

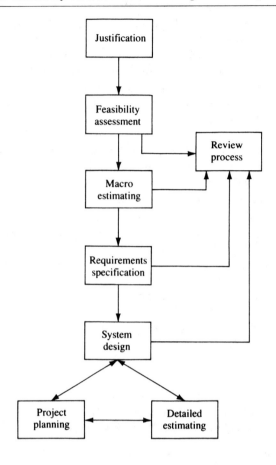

Papaccio (32) suggest the use of a software productivity improvement opportunity tree which pinpoints the major ways in which software cost savings can be achieved. However, this is not just a matter of identifying areas suitable for simple cost cutting but more a matter of focusing software engineering attention on overall improvements in the way software development projects are undertaken. The six major items proposed by Boehm and Papaccio are as follows:

Making people more effective

Providing incentives, training and facilities to encourage more effective working, not just faster production of software.

Making steps more effective

Design methodologies and software tools need to be made more effective by using them as part of an integrated project support environment (IPSE).

Eliminating steps

Automated aids often enable previous manual steps to be eliminated. More advanced approaches include domain-specific and domain-independent automatic programming facilities.

Eliminate rework

The use of requirements and design language oriented systems in conjunction with software design aids will eliminate a great deal of rework arising from ambiguity, omission and errors at the specification and design stages.

Build simpler products

Rapid prototyping and improved software process models can be very effective in designing and building simpler products which improve the overall productivity of the system development process.

Reuse components

Writing less code is an important consideration in improving productivity. The simplest approach is the development and *use* of a library of software components. However, this can be extended to become an effective applications generator if conventions and standards are specified and used for reusable software.

The ideas of Gilb and Boehm and Papaccio are moving away from the conventional waterfall approach to software definition, design and development. Greater emphasis is being placed on the broader-based examination of requirements and how that need can be most effectively satisfied. The waterfall approach places far too much emphasis on meeting rigidly defined functionality without sufficient attention being focused on effective construction. For the future more attention needs to be given to the overall cost effectiveness rather than simply meeting a specific short-term requirement. The process of evolutionary development and review covering feasibility, macroestimating, requirements specification and system design should be considered as the most useful approach to software development. In particular the emphasis must be on the following:

- An unambiguous definition of what is required.
- A clear understanding of how that can be provided as functional facilities for the end users.
- A clear understanding of how the system can be constructed.

One outcome of this approach will be the elimination of much high-cost gold plating in present systems — the inclusion of functionality that is superfluous to effectiveness. The focus and emphasis must be on not only understanding the requirement but also, and equally important, understanding the software costs.

Again it must be emphasised that cost cutting and cost saving are not the objectives; indeed, they are likely to be counter productive in this approach. The objective is to produce the best possible software system to meet the user's requirement in the most cost effective way. It is also essential to this approach that the link between system design, construction (project planning) and costing is set up at a very early stage in the project.

2.6   Planned installation

In addition to these new development strategies, consideration needs to be given to phased installation particularly where the system is to be used by a large number of people. Two situations should be considered at the feasibility stage:

1. Installation of the basic system followed at intervals by additional facilities. This may be appropriate where it is essential to replace an existing system but the timescale for development of all the new facilities is longer than desirable. The basic system can replace the existing system on a shorter timescale and then be followed later by the enhancements.

   This approach can also be used when piloting a new system, or where the investment is large and there is a need to start generating benefit from the system as early as possible in the investment profile.

   Experience shows that this approach is attractive to users and to senior management. It is also an approach that is easy to accommodate in design and development and as such is good software engineering practice. A phased approach to system development and installation should always be set out in the project plan and budget when seeking approval for a project.

2. Phased installation, where the system is to be used by a number of user groups or at a number of geographic locations. Consideration needs to be given at an early stage to the installation programme, firstly to identify a suitable site for introducing the system that minimises disruption to normal operations, and secondly to develop a planned order of sites that yields the highest return on the investment. From the author's experience on three major and diverse projects it was evident that the overall value of the system was significantly influenced by the installation sequence. These particular projects involved:

   (a) seven health care sites in which the mainframe computer was replaced and simultaneously four operational software systems were standardised between sites;

   (b) eighteen centres in four countries in which a new system for wharehousing and distribution replaced five different packages used across these sites;

   (c) eight oil production fields where a new maintenance system replaced two existing systems.

In each case the installation of the system and training of users took about 2 years and considerable effort was devoted to examining the order in which the sites were brought on to the system with particular emphasis on:

(a) selecting the most suitable initial site;
(b) deciding the order of installation at the other sites to achieve the best cash flow profile

2.7   Evaluating alternatives

The software industry has not yet matured to the point where significant reuse can be made of existing software, either at program or module level. However, this is likely to attract a great deal more attention over the next decade with the development and use of libraries of software components. This approach already has a strong and growing following in areas where mathematical and statistical routines are used and for industrial process systems. In the more general area of software the choice at present is usually between:

- A package, where one exists in the market.
- A bespoke development, based on core software or modification of an existing package.
- A custom development, based on a new specification.

For the future the latter two options are likely to merge and systems may well be built up by using a mix of software components in a customised software framework. At present, however, the first two options are very often ignored in a feasibility study. Packages are often quite wrongly seen as an expensive alternative to development from scratch, but in terms of the investment profile they can be more attractive as they provide proven software, available for use, on a much shorter timescale. The benefit from the use of this software can start to be gained much sooner. However, it must also be acknowledged that buying a package may involve a higher level of risk in terms of meeting the user's needs and the overall functional integrity of the system. Nevertheless it really is very important to evaluate packages as an alternative to a custom development in terms of the overall investment. An example which illustrates this point quite vividly is given below:

Example

Two potential customers in the same industrial sector with a maintenance operation on approximately the same size of plant, were offered an application package to run on existing DEC VAX hardware.

Customer A decided to go ahead with the purchase of the package after considering a custom development. At the outset a number of enhancements were commissioned as well as a user training programme. The overall costs were as follows:

Purchase of package	£100,000
Enhancements and training	£50,000
Total initial cost	£150,000

The system was enhanced, installed and loaded with data and staff trained within 6 months. Within a further 6 months significant operational savings were being made from the use of the maintenance information and subsequently the direct saving was about £1 million per year.

Customer B decided the package on offer was too expensive and sought an alternative proposal to develop a system on a PC. The software development was commissioned on the expectation that it would be operational within 6 months. After initial commissioning the shortcomings of the software became very apparent. These were largely due to the inexperience of maintenance engineers which was reflected directly in the specification: 'We will not need all of the refinements included in those expensive packages, all we need are the basic facilities.'

Inevitably more development was needed to include quite a few of the previously rejected 'refinements' and, typically, these extended the original specification and cost estimate by an order of magnitude. Furthermore the demands of the software enhancements were too great for the original hardware which also needed upgrading. The overall costs in this case were as follows:

Initial cost, including purchase of PC	£45,000
Subsequent development and additional hardware	£80,000
Total cost over 9 months	£125,000

Despite the additional investment the system was operationally unsatisfactory and it was abandoned after about a year and users continued with a manual system. The 'net benefit' was a *cost of £125,000* and a user group left with a very sceptical view of the value of IT.

The software industry is littered with examples of unsatisfactory developments which should never have been embarked on if a feasibility study had been carried out prior to making any commitment. Many of these unsatisfactory cases could have been turned into very worthwhile developments with a little more attention to the evaluation of alternatives and the identification of a viable option. However, it is important to acknowledge that packages are not the answer to all situations as by their very nature they are targeted at routine functions such as payroll, maintenance, accounts or materials control. For what may be described as non-routine activities it may be possible to use core software or system designs from other sources as an alternative to a complete custom development.

Custom-developed software should always be seen as potentially the most expensive route and should only be pursued when there is not a satisfactory alternative.

One argument for rejecting the package solution, apart from misconceptions on cost discussed in the foregoing, is the recurring cry 'we don't do it that way'. It is a defence used by those who cannot embrace change and only really want to continue to use the computer to put 'wheels under an existing manual system'. Unfortunately this still occurs all too often and custom development is being used in situations where there is no financial justification for that option and other options have not been explored.

In the 1960s the argument was applied to payroll software and many organisations spent large sums developing their own package to process payrolls *their own special way*.

In the 1970s project planning was the topic and there was a huge proliferation of packages. Many conferences were organised to discuss at some length the theme of how 'I did it my way'.

The 1980s has seen the development of hundreds of application software systems for a wide range of engineering, administrative and commercial uses and also the birth of the expensive colour graphics glossy, the executive information system. Developing packages of this kind without relating them to user activities and without a major shift in user practices and procedures is a complete waste of investment.

What, one wonders, will be the flavour of the 1990s? There are signs that it may be document handling and document management systems.

Some of the reinventing of the wheel in specific application areas can be attributed to the rapid development of IT and the consequent growing pains associated with the coming to maturity. However, with no sign yet of being in a position to produce software by other than manpower-intensive means, then software costs, overall, will remain high and will increase in direct proportion to the increase in salary of software engineers. In these circumstances every effort must be made to commission software in the most cost effective way and this includes avoiding the huge amount of duplication and wasteful development that occurs at present. The establishment of libraries of component software is one practical way in which software costs will be significantly reduced but only if these new facilities are considered early in the project cycle. It is at the feasibility stage that much of the present duplication and the associated high costs could be prevented by the rigorous evaluation of alternatives to a custom development.

2.8   Investment profiles

It is not sufficient just to estimate the cost of a software development. It is important to know the timescale over which those costs will be incurred and equally important to know the timescale over which the planned benefits will be realised. This does not need to be done in detail initially but simply as an order of cost over financial periods — months, quarters, half years, etc. — to provide senior management with a basis on which to make a decision about the proposed investment.

In Table 2.1 a macro estimate is given for a custom system development and the alternative of a package solution for the replacement of a CAD/CAM system. The total cost for the custom development is £108,000 and the purchase of a package is £240,000. In both cases there was an initial assessment cost of £10,000. Both options are expected to give a saving of £400,000 annually after a 6 months' settling-down period made up as given in Table 2.2 and assumed to be evenly

Table 2.1 Macro estimate for options

Item	Custom development	Purchase of package
Initial assessment	10,000	10,000
Requirements definition	6,000	5,000
Software tools	3,000	—
Design	25,000	—
Development	35,000	—
Implementation	11,000	13,000
Training	4,000	5,000
Project management	9,000	2,000
Operational software	15,000	215,000
Total initial costs	£118,000	£250,000
Support:		
Operational software — annual	2,000	25,000
Maintenance	8,000	—
Annual costs	£10,000	£25,000

Table 2.2 Initial assessment of benefit

Item	Benefit per year
Increased production	360,000
Saving in manpower	50,000
Saving in IT costs	20,000
Increased materials and parts	(20,000)
Total annual benefit	£400,000

spread over the year. The basis on which the estimate of cost and benefit is prepared is set out in Chapters 4 and 6.

On the face of it the custom development looks attractive at less than half the cost of the package. Indeed in many instances the decision to go ahead is made entirely on the comparison of the total costs and no assessment is made of the cash flow over the relevant timescale. However, the cost profiles and cash flow profiles for the two options, given in Tables 2.3 and 2.4, show that the package solution can be operational in a much shorter period and yield the expected benefits on a short timescale. The major drawback to the package solution is that the maximum negative cash flow is double that for the custom development and management will need to address the question of whether that is an acceptable up-front investment. The most useful comparative information for management decision purposes is the summary of the costs and benefits given in Table 2.5.

In this example only the basic cost and benefit figures have been used but, as mentioned in Section 1.6, opportunity cost must also be taken into account. As a matter of routine there should be an addition of interest, at the highest prevailing rate, to the costs over the period of negative cash flow. In addition, for projects that run beyond one fiscal year it is sensible, when comparing optional ways of implementing the system, to carry out a discounted cash flow (DCF) calculation

Table 2.3 Cash flow profile for custom development

Elapsed time (months)	3	6	9	12	15	18	21	24	27	30	33	36
Development cost (TIC)	10	8	25	40	20	15						
Support cost							5	5	5	5	5	5
Cost profile	10	8	25	40	20	15	5	5	5	5	5	5
Benefit profile									40	60	100	100
Cash flow profile	(10)	(18)	(43)	(83)	(103)	(118)	(123)	(128)	(93)	(38)	57	152

Table 2.4 Cash flow profile for purchase of package

Elapsed time (months)	3	6	9	12	15	18	21	24	27	30	33	36
Package cost (TIC)	10	240										
Support costs					25				25			
Cost profile	10	240			25				25			
Benefit profile				40	60	100	100	100	100	100	100	100
Cash flow profile	(10)	(250)	(250)	(210)	(175)	(75)	25	125	200	300	400	500

Table 2.5 Summary comparison of options

Item	Custom development	Purchase of package
Total cost	£118,000	£250,000
Maximum negative cash flow	£128,000	£250,000
Payback from commissioning	15 months	12 months
Payback from commitment	33 months	21 months
Annual ongoing return	£400,000	£400,000
Net benefit over 36 months	£152,000	£500,000

and then use a single figure, net present value (NPV), as the basis of comparing the options.

Software impinges on all aspects of business activity. In most situations a particular system is likely to have a direct financial benefit and this can be quantified and set against the development cost. In other situations the focus may be in intangible areas covering aspects of the business such as compliance, safety or security. What has to be assessed in these cases is the likely penalty, expressed in cost terms, of *not* proceeding and of course the timescale over which that cost would occur. The saving of those 'penalty' costs becomes the benefit from having the system. Software to protect against, or detect, software viruses is another area. Each business needs to look carefully at all aspects of the working environment and identify the particular needs in this respect.

2.9 An objective assessment before commitment

Far too many decisions about computer software are left to technical staff and to people low down in the organisation. Senior management often shun involvement on some curious pretext that they do not understand 'all this high-tech'. Those same people probably know little about the workings of the internal combustion engine but make satisfactory investment decisions about vehicles for company transport purposes.

Everyone involved should take an objective view of software investment at the feasibility study stage, keeping in mind the principal points on which the justification was based:

- What is needed?
- How can it be provided?
- What will it cost?
- What will be the benefit?

If an objective approach is followed and data is set out in a consistent way then any subsequent changes such as variations in the design, project timescale, etc., can be costed and compared with the feasibility study figures. Any agreed change in the budget commitment can be based on a revised cost and investment profile that is easily understood. Even decisions on replacement systems should be subject to the same procedure and should include an audit of benefit derived from the existing system. This is discussed in more detail in Chapter 10, in dealing with life cycle costing.

2.10   Assessing the requirement

At the outset of a new development there is not likely to be a detailed specification available and whatever form of specification or statement of requirements is available, it may be modified in the light of more detailed consideration. Nevertheless, management will require an overall estimate of cost before approving further action or making preliminary budget provision. 'Ballpark' figures tend to be just that and are often plucked out of thin air. The focus in estimating software costs, even at this early stage, must be to use an objective basis. The first step is therefore to assess the relevance of the following and the overall size of the project in terms of effort and cost:

- Is it a new application area?
- Is it a replacement of an existing system?
- Will the system have to interface to existing facilities?
- Are there system security requirements?

It is also necessary even at this early stage of software planning to establish the life cycle requirements of the particular software being considered and the implications this may have in terms of design constraints. These must be taken into account in assessing the initial cost. As will be seen later, in Chapter 10, software with the most cost effective life cycle may not be the lowest cost option from the standpoint of the initial development.

Overall size is broadly defined in Table 2.6 but in individual cases the relationship between duration, effort and cost may be quite different from those given in the table.

Table 2.6 Overall size classification for systems

Size	Duration in months	Effort in man years	Development cost in £ sterling
Small	6	1	70,000
Medium	20	30	900,000
Large	30	150	5,000,000
Very large	60	400	10,000,000

The size of the project has a bearing on the amount of administration involved — above 5 man years' effort there must be a full-time effort committed to the project. This is additional to the effort required for technical leadership of the project. Size, expressed in these parameters, is also useful to management as it gives an indication of the level of financial commitment and exposure.

2.11 Identifying particular development features

In addition to assessing the size of the requirement it is also important to identify features that will influence the development effort, the value of the operational system and the potential life cycle including the following:

- Degree of new technology. Where a lot is involved the risk will be correspondingly high.
- Degree of innovation in method and techniques. This may be impressive but at the risk of failing to provide users with effective facilities.
- Compatibility with existing software. This should not be a constraint on the life cycle of the new software.
- Modularity for life cycle development. This will allow parts to be replaced easily and at low cost as needs change over the life cycle of the system.
- Special features such as safety critical software or high-integrity systems. These are likely to permeate more widely in the future.

2.12 Selecting a base for comparison

Techniques and models for estimating will be dealt with in the following chapters. However, the key to all estimating methods is to draw on past work and use what is known and dependable as a basis for future estimates. It will suffice to say here that the quality of estimates and the quality of project management are quite independent and the various combinations of quality will lead to the expectations of cost estimating and cost control as set out in Table 2.7.

All of the models developed for software costing need to be calibrated in the user's environment and depend on parametric values derived from past work. It is therefore important to establish a broad picture of the requirement, and the development features, so that it is possible to identify relevant parameter values that match the proposed development to a reasonable degree and provide a good

Table 2.7 Expectations of quality from available data

Quality of estimates	Quality of project management	Expectation of good cost control	Value for future cost estimating
Good	Good	High	Good
Good	Poor	Fair	Fair
Poor	Good	Low	Low
Poor	Poor	Very poor	Doubtful

base for estimating. In situations where there is no established estimating database it is useful to follow a disciplined approach and to make use of a simple systematic model such as the analog model; see Chapter 3 and Appendix II.

2.13   An objective view of estimates

Contingency has not yet been mentioned in the context of estimating. It is a favourite resort of all those who do not or will not use a systematic approach to estimating. It is usually used as an arbitrary add-on because of the following:

- Uncertainty about a particular technical area.
- Concern that something has been omitted.
- Concern that something has been underestimated.

The whole area of uncertainty is dealt with in Chapter 4, and in Chapter 5 the inclusion of contingency is discussed in the context of the plan of execution. However, before moving on it is important in setting out a basis of objective estimating to say that adding 10%, 20% or even 50% for contingency to a macro estimate does nothing to improve the value or quality of the estimate, nor will it do anything to increase confidence in the cost of the proposed system. Indeed it has quite the reverse effect because it clearly demonstrates that those responsible do not know what they are doing. Instead of using the blunt instrument of contingency in this way it is much more constructive if each of the above aspects is dealt with in an objective way.

If there is a perceived **technical risk** involved in the proposed project then time and effort must be focused on evaluating the risk and identifying ways in which the risk can be minimised. At the same time the procedure must be to identify and cost the alternative, or fallback, techniques. The option of longest duration and highest cost should be identified and if appropriate the cost estimate for the high-risk and low-risk option should be put forward, together with the corresponding estimate of potential benefit.

If it is thought that **something has been omitted** then a thorough reappraisal of the tasks and requirements of the project should be carried out. Adding 10% contingency to a £50,000 estimate will be of little help if someone has failed to include the cost of £10,000 for a DBMS licence!

Finally, **underestimating** is a natural hazard of all planning and costing activities. There is no quick-fix solution — a re-examination of the estimates is necessary, focusing particularly on the areas of suspected weakness and uncertainty. A second-pass iteration should be carried out to increase confidence in the built-up estimate. Where possible a separate estimate can be made using another previous development as a base. There may be differences between the two built-up costs. If the difference is significant then a detailed assessment must be made identifying where these differences are arising so that there is a basis for getting convergence. To carry out comparative estimating in this way will of course depend on the availability of more than one suitable base system to draw upon, but it is worth doing even if the match of the second base is not particularly good. However, there will not be particularly good convergence in this situation.

Above all else, remember at all stages that estimating is a process of improvement of the project cost by iteration and that at the early stage of assessing justification and examining feasibility the objective is to establish an order of magnitude cost in which both management and technical staff can have a reasonable degree of confidence.

3 Software estimating methods and models

3.1 General observations on software models

There are over 20 methods and models for software cost estimating documented in the literature. Some of these date back to the early 1970s and are not relevant now; others have been developed and refined to meet the ever growing demand for improving the estimation of software project costs. These models employ a wide variety of methods and require a wide range of input factors, but the output from the majority of these models is an estimation of manpower effort. This is subsequently converted to costs by the use of a manpower unit cost as a follow-through process. Some older models, that now get little public airing, were based on software costs estimated as a proportion of hardware costs. That was at a time when software costs were less than 40% of the total system costs and hardware was the dominant factor. This type of model has no relevance to accurate software costing because hardware costs have come down by several orders of magnitude; software costs have continued to rise in line with inflation and now amount to about 90% of the total cost to the end user over the life cycle of the software.

Most models are based on a methodology that involves an analytical formula relating the output to a number of inputs. The output, as mentioned above, is a measure of the effort required, based on the number of parametric inputs defining the system characteristics, system size, complexity, and development environment. These main parameters are usually referred to as cost drivers as they are the factors which influence the development cost. These models cannot, however, be used as an instant solution for estimating any software development. Firstly there are basic limitations — some models cannot be used for programs with less than 2,000 lines of code and one is limited to projects not exceeding 5 years' duration. The latter constraint is unlikely to worry the majority of us — unless we overrun by a significant degree! However, the lower-level limit must be considered as a serious restriction at a time when the software industry is aiming for a high level of modularity with relatively small programs in each module. Secondly these models, whilst acknowledging factors such as software complexity as a necessary input, have widely varying definitions of complexity and hence widely varying parametric values for taking these factors into account. Nevertheless these models have each been developed to meet a particular need and have had some degree of success in that particular environment.

3.2 Characteristics of models

The two most important characteristics of software costing models to the practitioner are **approach** and **usefulness** which are discussed in the following.

(i) Top-down approach

This approach gives an overall cost estimate based on the global properties of the proposed system. It is a natural and logical approach and allows costing to follow the evolutionary approach to design and development — starting from the conceptual stage and moving on to more detail as the system definition progresses and subsystems are identified.

The major disadvantage to the top-down approach is that difficult technical problems, which would be evident at detail level, may be overlooked in the early, more global, stage of estimating. It is these technical design aspects that are likely to cause significant escalation of the costs at later stages and it is therefore crucial that a technical feasibility study is done at the very beginning of the project and that re-evaluation of technical feasibility continues as the design progresses. This gives increased understanding of the system structure and complexity and will be reflected in the detail of the cost estimate. In the top-down approach the cost estimate evolves in detail and accuracy with the definition of the major parts of the system, and the cost of the system as a whole is available from an aggregation of these parts. At any stage of development a representative cost estimate can be obtained. The advantage of the top-down approach is that the structure of the estimate relates directly to software engineering design practices, project planning and control, and furthermore the structure of the estimate can be used directly as the basis for cost control purposes.

(ii) Bottom-up approach

This approach involves the costing of software components in the form that they will be developed — related to the work breakdown structure. This implies a high degree of accuracy and often appeals to those becoming involved in costing from a background of software development. Indeed, bottom-up estimating is often undertaken by people with a detailed understanding of the work involved. However, there is some danger of estimates for component parts of the software being done on a 'personal' basis related to the individual's skill and productivity, thus introducing a level of personal bias that can be misleading in building up the estimate. The main drawback of the bottom-up approach is that it cannot be done until there is a well-defined design and the nature and size of the components are known. Detailed data needed for estimating is often not available in the early stages of a project and the bottom-up approach cannot therefore be used at the conceptual stage. Nevertheless it is important to use the skill and understanding of technical specialists to assess size and complexity and hence feasibility at the conceptual stage, but this can often best be channelled through prototyping which is aimed at more complex parts of the system.

The bottom-up approach is therefore complementary to the top-down approach and although as an overall basis for a model it is not particularly attractive, it can be used as a valuable part of the overall methodology of sizing and cost estimating.

(iii)   Usefulness

'Usefulness' may at first sight seem to lack objectivity in any discussion of costing models, but software design and software costing methods are changing and it is necessary to consider the suitability of models in this context taking particular account of the following:

Adaptability

Is the model suitable for use in a changing environment? Can it be updated to incorporate new analytical techniques and software development methods?

Flexibility

Can it be used for macro *and* detailed estimates? Is it usable (with suitable calibration) in a variety of software environments — real time, mathematical modelling or transaction processing? Also, does it allow intervention and adaptation of the input parameters and cost drivers?

Efficiency

Is the model process easy to learn and is the model easy to use?

Based on these criteria of usefulness it is interesting to examine some of the reviews made of major models produced over the last two decades. One example is a comparative assessment cited by Cover (5). Using a well-documented software development as a base, estimates of output from six models showed a variation from 6,600 lines of code to over 37,000 lines of code compared with the actual 9,000 lines of code. Another example is that given by Mohanty (6) in which 11 models were used to estimate the cost of a hypothetical system of fixed size. The results gave a range of costs varying from $325,000 to $2,750,000 — in all cases the manpower unit-cost rate was the same. Kemerer (7) has also published the results of an empirical evaluation of a range of software cost estimation models. He used a selection of projects, carried out by a software house, which was considered to be a reasonably consistent development environment. Comparisons of the model output with the actual effort showed a great deal of inconsistency between models for a given project and for a given model across all 15 projects. The results showed a variation from actual ranging from 85% to over 700%.

In all of these assessments the authors are quick to point out that it is not the accuracy of the models that is being called into question but that they have been used outside their original environment, probably without sufficient attention to calibration and tuning. However, the variation in the results mentioned above clearly indicates the need to calibrate a model for use in a specific organisation and this is likely to require a lot of effort and time without any certainty of a successful outcome. Indeed, Bailey and Basili (8) are quite explicit on the matter of transportability and suggest

> that due to the great variability of factors influencing software projects in different organisations, no cost models are truly transportable between environments; ultimately there can be no useful generic model. That does not mean that organisations should abandon software prediction but rather that each should examine its own environment carefully and produce or calibrate a model suited to its own requirements.

Potential users would therefore need to be confident that a particular model was well suited to the needs of the organisation before a major investment was made in setting it up and regarding it as a reliable tool.

3.3   Selecting a model

In most models the output is focused on the software development process but it is necessary to know to what extent the main activities and work components are covered. The 'region of fit' for a model should, as a minimum, be assessed against the following:

- System specification.
- Software design.
- Software development.
- System testing.
- Installation and acceptance.
- Documentation.

Quinnan (9) gives a useful list of work components and outputs for these main activities against which a model can be assessed, but operational support should be excluded when considering models primarily aimed at estimating for software development.

It is also important to ensure that the cost estimating model is matched to the design approach and to the tools — particularly fourth-generation languages (4GLs) — to be used for software development.

Calibration of the model is an important consideration at the selection stage as it directly affects the usefulness of the model in the chosen environment as mentioned above. Calibration is only effective if sufficient attention is given to data collection and indeed, if sufficient, satisfactory information is available from which to derive good-quality calibration parameters. Cover (5) points out that data collection for all models is an essential part of the pre-operational investment and requires that:

— a structure for data collection be set up which must directly map with cost driver elements of the model to be used.
— a mechanism must be established for maintaining the database and making it readily accessible to potential users.

Cover goes on to point out 'that data collection is neither trivial nor free and any organisation unwilling to make the necessary investment in data collection will not be able to make any better estimates than they can without a model or methodology'.

Moreover, the investment in data collection will only be justified if there is a full commitment to using the model. It must also be borne in mind that improvement in forward estimating will not be instantaneous; it will be an evolutionary process, geared not only to the investment in retrospective analysis but also to continuous forward adjustment.

This leads on to the second major aspect concerning the effectiveness of models, namely the factors which affect software development productivity and how well the models represents these factors. The originator of the model may have taken a particular view on this and taken account of productivity in a certain way. This may not suit the target organisation but it may not be practical to change the form of the parameters used.

The use of an estimating model involves a medium- to longer-term commitment — certainly it is not a short-term solution. The software industry and software engineering techniques are characterised by change — often radical. These may seem irreconcilable factors which make the goal of improved and reliable estimating unattainable. It is the author's view that a hybrid approach will need to be developed which is flexible and allows the user to include the features appropriate to the particular needs of the situation. This is discussed further in Chapter 4 under the total installed cost (TIC) approach where the output from any model is considered as a source of information contributing to the cost estimating process.

Consistency and compatibility are necessary from the initial macro estimates through detailed estimating, cost control of the project and for retrospective project review. It is important to choose an approach that will meet these requirements. In the following sections some modelling approaches are discussed with particular emphasis on their suitability for macro estimating at the conceptual stage, as well as for detailed cost estimating at the specification and design stage and for interfacing with project cost control.

3.4   Analog models

Estimation by analogy provides a systematic, simple and effective approach to cost estimating. The method is based on the comparison of a proposed software development project with one or more previous projects carried out in the same organisation and for which the costs are known and understood. The analog model can be used at macro-level to give a global estimate in the early stages of development and then refined as the design process progresses. A very simple macro-level model in which a limited number of parameters are used has a great deal of merit as a starting point for cost estimating when no other method can be applied due to the absence of suitable data. The basis of the model process is to identify a past project that is considered to be the best match with the proposed project and to adjust that base for differences in complexity, skill, size and other factors which are considered likely to influence the cost of the proposed project relative to the base project. This is a very basic and empirical approach to cost estimating but has the virtue that it imposes some discipline on the estimating procedure.

The number of parameters can be chosen to suit the situation and to make use of the particular data available. There are obvious dangers associated with a rather random approach to comparative estimation based on 'differences' from a base, and the analog approach is normally used in an orderly way where factors that are considered to constitute cost drivers are selected from a predefined checklist. The validity of the analog approach does depend on the closeness of match between the proposed project and the base system and requires a very clear assessment of the 'differences' and their relevance as cost drivers. Cowderoy and Jenkins (10) emphasise the following as important if a satisfactory estimate is to be made:

• That the overall size and purpose of the previous product are roughly similar to those of the proposed new one.
• That the overall method of working in the previous project is similar to that of the new project.
• That there are either very detailed records about the work, or people available who remember it accurately.

The latter point is questionable because people have poor retention even over relatively short periods. However, it is important to make use of every source of data, and in any case the final judgement on the estimate will be made by someone with experience in estimating.

A refinement to the analog approach is the formulation of a checklist of modifiers against which the differences between the base and the proposed project can be assessed. In this respect the simple model then becomes parameter based using percentage difference 'modifiers', from the base, to arrive at an estimated cost for the new system. If this method is to be used repeatedly then post-project reviews are essential to build up a suitable database on which to validate the different modifiers.

The analog model is discussed further in Appendix II. Whilst it has limitations in comparison with some other models it is useful in the following situations:

• Where there is no estimating methodology in place.
• Where there is some past project information but no detailed historical database.
• Where a quick, easy and reasonably accurate macro estimate is required (given the proviso above of reasonable match between base and proposal).

A further refinement to the analog model method is to prepare an estimate for a new project based on modules or subsystems taken from a number of past projects. This has merit when there is no single past project that is considered a good enough match with the proposed project and where parts of other projects match well with the requirement.

3.5   Algorithmic models

The algorithmic models, often using mathematical algorithms, are perhaps regarded by many as true models and other approaches more as methods. The basis of most analytical models is a formulation of the type:

$$MM = aL^b$$

where MM is man months of effort and

L is lines of code

Many of the models under this heading are referred to as SLOC (Source Lines of Code) models or sometimes KSLOC or DSI (Delivered Source Instructions) or KDSI (K = thousand).

The need for a careful choice of model and the need to calibrate thoroughly are evident when account is taken of the foregoing and the realisation that for this group of models:

a varies from about 2 to 5

b varies from about 0.4 to just over 5

Boehm (11) groups algorithmic models in the following way:

- Linear.
- Multiplicative.
- Analytic.
- Tabular.
- Composite.

He gives a description of these methods and a very detailed account of the use of COCOMO, perhaps the best known of the software costing models. Boehm also gives a useful comparison between nine other algorithmic models: SLIM; Doty; PRICE S; TRW Wolverton; IBM-FSD; Boeing; GRC; SDC and the Bailey and Basili Meta-Model.

Cowderoy and Jenkins (10) also give an assessment of COCOMO; SLIM; Bailey and Basili Meta-Model and COPMO (Conte *et al.* (12)), probably the latest (1986) of these types of models to be developed.

A fundamental part of the algorithmic method is focused on software sizing and the activities immediately relevant to the development process. The items that are considered to influence effort and hence cost are identified as cost drivers and are the basis on which the model variables are formulated. Boehm gives a

Table 3.1 Attributes used as cost drivers in various cost models

Group	Factor	SDC 1965	TRW 1972	Putnam SLIM	Doty	RCA PRICE S	IBM	Boeing 1977	GRC 1979	COCOMO
Size attributes	Source instructions	x			x		x	x		x
	Object instructions	x	x		x					
	Number of routines			x		x				
	Number of data items					x	x			x
	Number of output formats								x	
	Documentation				x		x	x		
	Number of personnel									
Program attributes	Type	x	x	x	x	x	x	x		
	Complexity		x			x	x	x		x
	Language	x		x				x	x	
	Reuse			x				x	x	x
	Required reliability					x				x
Computer attributes	Time constraints		x	x	x	x	x	x	x	x
	Storage constraints			x	x	x	x		x	x
	Hardware configuration	x				x				
	Concurrent hardware devel.	x			x	x	x			x
Personnel attributes	Personnel capability					x	x			x
	Personnel continuity						x			
	Hardware experience	x		x	x	x	x			x
	Applications experience		x	x		x	x	x	x	x
	Language experience			x		x	x		x	x
Project attributes	Tools and techniques			x		x	x	x		x
	Customer interface	x					x			
	Requirements definition	x			x	x	x			x
	Requirements volatility	x			x	x	x		x	x
	Schedule			x						
	Security						x			
	Computer access	x		x	x		x	x	x	x
	Travel/rehosting	x			x	x				

Source: Reproduced from Boehm (11) by kind permission of Prentice Hall Inc.

comparison of the attributes that are considered as cost drivers in these various models that were in use in the early 1980s (see Table 3.1).

Algorithmic models are useful in situations where there is a good parameter value database, available from past projects, and where design methods and design tools are reasonably consistent. It is not surprising therefore that the use of this type of model has been confined to very large organisations. A particular operational weakness of these models is the significant overhead in setting up the model and calibrating it to a target software engineering environment. Another weakness is the unsuitability to small-scale development and to estimating for the enhancement, or restructuring, of existing software.

Algorithmic models have the great advantage of objectivity and consistency and the output is not subject to personal influence. However, as Boehm quite rightly states, 'like any other model, there is no way the (algorithmic) model can compensate for poor sizing and inaccurate cost driver ratings'.

The algorithmic models are important in large-scale software development environments and must not be dismissed lightly, but some of the factors that must be considered carefully before committing to this approach are as follows:

1. Code size is becoming less relevant as a guide to effort and of course cost in the software development process particularly where 4GLs are used and in CASE-oriented development environments.
2. Executable lines of code are not usually comparable, in terms of development effort, with other code such as data definition, comments, etc. Furthermore the increase in on-line help facilities and user documentation will have an influence on the manpower effort required to produce a 'delivered system' compared with historic records for comparable systems.
3. Counting delivered code takes no account of the actual developed lines of code. Some code may be discarded, some may be changed arising from changes in the specification after the initial design and estimate. All of this requires effort and cost which may not be reflected satisfactorily in a measure of the delivered lines of code.
4. Code size only applies to parts of the software development effort and in addition there are significant costs incurred in software development that cannot be reflected by measures of code size or productivity. Consequently this type of model provides an estimate for only part of the total software cost.

3.6   Function point models

Function metrics were first discussed by Albrecht (13) in 1979 and subsequently by Albrecht and Gaffney (14) and by Behrens (15). Further development of the method has been done by Low and Jeffery (33) and by Symons (34).

The objective in the function point method is to develop a relative measure of the function value delivered to the user that is independent of the particular technology or approach used. Function point models use program entities as sizing parameters and in broad terms cover user facilities and processing complexity. The general approach is based on counting the following:

- External inputs.
- External outputs.
- Logical internal files.
- External interface files.
- External enquiry.

These counts are weighted to reflect the function value to the customer and the weights recommended by Albrecht are classified as simple, average or complex with the following values:

	Simple	Average	Complex
External input	×3	×4	×6
External output	×4	×5	×7
Logical internal file	×7	×10	×15
External interface file	×5	×7	×10
External enquiry	×3	×4	×6

The sum of the weighted counts represents the unadjusted function points (UFP). The weighted sum is also adjusted for complexity by considering these items individually. The original figures given by Albrecht seem on the face of it rather too simple to reflect a wide range of complexity. Symons has focused on this aspect and proposed the use of a technical complexity factor determined by weighting 14 characteristics according to the *degree of influence* they each have in a particular software development project. These general application characteristics are as follows:

Data communications	On-line update
Distributed functions	Complex processing
Performance	Reusability
Heavily used configuration	Installation ease
Transaction rate	Operational ease
On-line data entry	Multiple sites
End user efficiency	Facilitate change

The technical complexity factor (TCF) = $0.65 + 0.01 \times DI$ where DI is the sum of the weighted degree of influence.

The system size in function points (FP) is expressed as:

$$FP = UFP \times TCF$$

Function points are therefore a dimensionless number providing a relative measure of the system size which is independent of development environment factors but specific to the technology, particularly the programming language, used in the development.

One advantage of the function point method is that the system components can be identified and quantified early in the project and it gives a good basis for macro estimating. System size can subsequently be refined in step with the definition of the functional specification and the design process.

The output from the function point method is essentially a system size estimate and when divided by the number of hours required for production gives a measure of productivity for future estimating purposes. These figures are of course limited to estimating for projects where the software tools and environment are the same as the base projects from which they were derived. Within an organisation with well-defined procedures and technology the function point method provides an effective approach to estimating the size and effort for software development aspects of a project. One weakness, however, is that if new technology is introduced then a complete recalibration of productivity is necessary. Even when this has been done there is still a need for great caution in subsequent estimating. Function point models can, however, be used in conjunction with, and fully complemented by, formal prototyping procedures to give additional data for new requirements. Where a comparable recent example is not available, the procedure to follow is to build the function, assess the effort and timescale, and then pro rata for the number of occurrences in the new system.

The particular strengths of a function point model are that it is applicable in the following cases:

- Throughout the range from small-scale to large-scale software development projects.
- To development, enhancement and re-engineering.
- To customisation of packages and core software.

However, the method has only been developed for use with business applications and would need to be completely restructured for use with real-time and mathematical applications because of the totally different internal structure and complexity of these types of software.

3.7   Prototyping as a model for estimating

Prototyping has not yet been used to full effect in the software industry. It has been used to a certain extent for system specification and for a range of exploratory purposes. It has the potential to become a valuable aid in estimating particularly in circumstances where there is little data on which to base an estimate. One such instance is where new software tools are to be used for a development; then prototyping could be used to calibrate productivity. There is also scope to use prototyping as a means of generating data for the function point model in situations where there is no relevant data available.

3.8   Other methods and models

New approaches to the task of estimating will always be coming forward and these should be encouraged and tried out where appropriate. Cowderoy and Jenkins (10) propose a new estimation tool that combines the merits of the algorithmic approach with a spreadsheet approach. The estimation modelling language (EML-1) would interface to a workbench database and also be able to interface to expert systems.

Expert systems have a long way to go before they will make any significant impact on software cost estimating, simply because of the diverse nature of past and future projects and also the fact that expert views and judgements are diverse and can be biased in a number of ways — optimism, pessimism, desire to win, desire to please, etc. The other important aspects that mitigate against an overdependence on experts are the following:

- People are not good stores of information; there is a tendency to forget or overlook detail even on a relatively short timescale.
- People do not know about all aspects of the total project and those who have a broad command of technical matters on past projects are unlikely to have much knowledge of the cost aspects.

Having said all that, though, the ultimate decision to accept and put forward a cost for a proposed project will always be based on the personal judgement of an experienced software engineer.

There is always scope for new models and methods but it is not a simple or quick way to establish an alternative to the methods discussed in the foregoing. DeMarco (3) supports the Bailey and Basili view that there are no transportable cost models but also that cost modelling is not irrelevant. However, the main requirements are a sufficient pool of data on past projects and a good deal of commitment — it is unlikely that the first 'model' formulation will produce a satisfactory result.

DeMarco put forward four major areas that need attention in formulating a cost model as follows:

1. Decomposition of costs.
2. Formulation of cost theory.
3. Data collection.
4. Statistical correlation.

These have been used as a basis for the following discussion on model development.

Decomposition of costs

It is necessary to break the costs of existing projects down into pieces that represent some part of the process. These must of course be parts of the software development process that can be built back up to give a built-up cost for the proposed project. In Chapter 4, in dealing with the total installed cost (TIC) template, a breakdown is given of the main activities, or elements, in software design and development and these could be used as a starting point for anyone considering the development of a model.

Formulation of cost theory

A causal relationship must be developed for the elements, or groups of elements, used in the decomposition. These should be confined, in the first instance, to fairly basic relationships such as linear, square root or *n* power. For example, it is not unreasonable to assume that effort and cost is a linear relationship for enquiry screens — the effort for the number needed in the prediction is related linearly to the effort needed for past numbers of enquiry screens.

However, it is not just the formal relationship that requires attention; there is the very complex issue of what are the appropriate number and mix of cost drivers to use. In the models already developed and mentioned earlier in this chapter, there have been in excess of 120 items used in various combinations, but most people agree that only a subset of the potential items should be considered and those should be restricted to items that can be quantified. This is unfortunate in that some of the factors that have the most impact on cost estimation and control are to do with the project team and as yet we have no way of effectively quantifying these items. These include team synergy — project manager, team interaction — and the variation in productivity that arises from the impact of project staffing which covers team structure, skill levels and turnover.

Before taking the development of a model any further it is strongly recommended that the reader looks at Section 6.5 and DeMarco and Lister (16).

Data collection

The pool of data referred to earlier should be decomposed and will be used to verify and then calibrate the formulation discussed above. Experience shows that this is likely to be a depressing process because the records will not yield information in a form required for the decomposition and there is no point in 'adjusting' or restructuring as this will be counter productive when it comes to the correlation of theory and practice. The most likely outcome is the conclusion that data will have to be collected from future projects before any effective use can be made of the prediction process. All of this points to the need for a much more disciplined approach to estimating and looking at a model development for a particular environment will highlight any weakness in the present process of estimating and post-project review.

Statistical correlation

A statistical method is used to establish the degree of fit between the costs theory and the sets of data. It will also yield values for constants in the cost equation but these will only be of use if the degree of fit, expressed as a standard error of estimation, is less than $\pm 25\%$.

The development of a model is not a static process. Project costs must be decomposed on an ongoing basis and the correlation repeated from time to time. Furthermore any significant change in the software design or development process

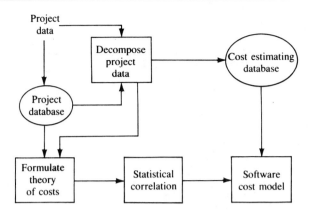

Figure 3.1
Development of a
software cost model

that will influence the effort, productivity and cost must be taken into account and this may involve a reformulation of the relationships of elements and a restructuring of the model. The process of developing and supporting the cost model is illustrated in Figure 3.1.

Despite what has been said in the foregoing, software engineers should not be discouraged from considering a cost model development but it should be confined to the area of software design and development and not attempt to be all embracing. Finally it is important to understand that there is no single model or method that will give a good prediction of software costs. The majority of people writing on the subject of software cost estimating agree on one important point — *good estimation is based on the understanding and use of a range of tools and techniques and the expert judgement as to which combinations are most appropriate in each situation.*

4 A systematic approach to estimating

4.1 Aims of estimating

The primary aims of the estimator are as follows:

1. To provide an estimate that is in a consistent format and can be understood by both technical and non-technical people. The need for consistency is to ensure that different options can be readily assimilated and assessed and that the effect of revision in the specification and any other changes that might affect the budget can be readily seen in cost terms.
2. To provide management with a stable and realistic estimate of cost for getting a software system operational. All too often estimates presented to management have to be revised upwards within a short timescale by 50% or 100% due solely to the *omission* of key elements of cost and *not* to poor estimating of the software coding aspects.
3. To provide an estimate in a format that can be related directly to project and cost control so that reports to management on progress are consistent with their original understanding of the cost make-up.

Another important requirement in preparing estimates is that they are compatible with the structure of cost reporting and post-project review so that the cost database is enhanced directly for future use without a lot of restructuring and *adjustment* (more will be said in Chapter 6 on this matter when 'output adjustment' to cost estimates is discussed).

In the past the software industry has had the opportunity to develop and install systems for 'new' application areas. The number of green-field opportunities is already diminishing and an increasing proportion of future work will be restructuring and re-engineering and the installation of replacement systems.

The methods and approaches developed for costing software must reflect the activities of the software industry as a whole and in particular the models and methods must embrace re-engineering and replacement as well as green-field development.

There is now a pressing need to identify the component elements of a comprehensive cost estimate, suited to the full range of requirements, if the IT industry is to move into a situation where cost estimation and control is set on a satisfactory and consistent footing. The main requirement is to formulate a basis for bringing the relevant data together from the various sources, be they estimating models or quotations for support software. Experience has shown that one way to establish a satisfactory basis that is systematic in approach is to use a costing template. This can be used as a checklist for compiling the cost elements and is also a good consistent basis for comparing the cost of optional solutions. Checklists themselves are tiresome, tedious and often so general that they are irrelevant to most practical situations. Users working through the checklist find they often have to omit large sections and eventually they ignore the whole document. Thus one consequence is that checklists can have the reverse effect of that desired. The template approach provides a framework for aggregating costs derived from estimating models, expert judgement and known or quoted costs which together represent a much more realistic estimate of the cost of installing a particular software system. Also, the template approach, when set up on a spreadsheet, provides an effective and rapid way of entering modifications and updates to the cost elements so that iterations can be incorporated and carried through to the full built-up costs in a single step.

4.2   Total installed cost approach

The basis of the total installed cost (TIC) template approach is the recognition that when management ask 'what is it going to cost?' they do not want half the story, and when they ask 'what are the alternatives?' they want a realistic comparative assessment of costed options, which again covers all the relevant items that need to be included in a prospective project budget.

The software estimating models discussed in Chapter 3 do not cover the whole cost framework but they do have an important contribution to make towards estimating some of the cost elements, and as such they are an important input to the TIC template. However, program coding, as such, now only accounts for some 20% of the total cost to set up an operational software system. Other major factors in estimating the cost of software are the definition of requirements, the design of the system and associated support structure, and implementation. Another important cost element is third-party software — such as CAD, DBMS, CASE tools and EXPERT system shells.

The TIC template is a simple model that aggregates costs from various sources:

- Estimates for software development.
- Quoted costs for third-party software.
- Project management.
- Data transfer.
- Training.

Where a formal model is not in use for estimating effort for coding and related tasks, estimates for the individual activities in that part of the project can be input directly to the TIC. The TIC is also the base for linking estimating and project planning so that a cost profile can be generated, and reiterated, that is wholly in step with the planned work schedule. The outputs from the TIC template are the following:

- An estimate of the total project cost.
- A cost profile over the timescale of the project.

The expected benefit from the operational use of the software can be combined with the TIC cost profile to give a cash flow profile. This provides management with essential information on which to assess the project viability and approve a budget. In particular the cash flow profile identifies the pattern of investment over the duration of the project and the timescale over which the benefits will be achieved and the investment justified. The advantage of the TIC template is that revision to the estimate of cost, or timescale, can be directly reflected in a revised cash flow profile.

The TIC template in the context of software cost estimating is illustrated in Figure 4.1.

The TIC approach is not confined to use with custom development software systems; it can be used for the full range of requirements as follows:

1. Estimating custom development.
2. Comparing custom development with other options.
3. Comparing the cost of packages.
4. Estimating the re-engineering of installed systems.

It has been used and proved to be an effective tool for all of these requirements.

Figure 4.1
TIC template in the cost estimating process

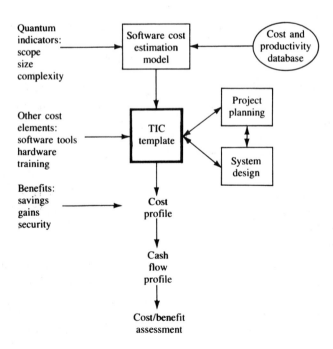

4.3   The TIC template

The TIC template consists of two levels of information — primary and secondary. The primary-level elements are given below and the secondary-level elements are discussed in the following sections of this chapter. The primary elements are as follows:

- Assessment.
- Requirements definition.
- Software tools.
- Hardware facilities for development.
- Design.
- Development.
- Implementation.
- Training.
- Project management and administration.
- Operational software.

There has been a marked shift in the contribution of these elements to overall software costs over the last 10 to 15 years and there is likely to be a further significant shift in the next decade. In Table 4.1 the distribution of total installed cost across the primary elements is given for the past (last 10 years), the present and the future (next 10 years). These are general distributions based on a range of projects and are included to illustrate the broad pattern of change. The significance of this table is to illustrate the importance of each element in estimating the true cost of software and to show the need for adaptability in estimating over the long term.

   The main purpose of the primary elements is to provide a defined set of headings under which costs are compiled to ensure consistency between the different estimates and demonstrate unequivocally what has been included or omitted.

Table 4.1   Average distribution of TIC across primary elements

Primary cost elements	Past	Present	Future
1. Assessment	2	12	15
2. Requirements definition	5	8	10
3. Software tools	2	10	20
4. H/W facilities for development	5	2	—
5. Design	30	20	20
6. Development	33	20	15
7. Implementation	15	10	5
8. Training	2	3	5
9. Project management	4	5	5
10. Operational software	2	10	5
Total Installed Cost	100%	100%	100%

Table 4.2 Total installed cost template — cost profile

Primary cost elements	Elapsed time from start										Total
	1	2	3	4	5	6	7	8	9	10	
Assessment											
Requirements definition											
Software tools											
H/W facilities for development											
Design											
Development											
Implementation											
Training											
Project management and administration											
Operational software											
Total installed cost (TIC)											

The cost profile for the project can be prepared based on the 10 primary elements and a spreadsheet for this purpose is given in Table 4.2. The elapsed timescale and units can be chosen to suit the particular project and can be in weeks, months or quarters as appropriate.

The secondary-level elements are the main checklist which guides the estimator to ensure that all relevant aspects have been covered in preparing the estimate. In practice it is necessary to set up tertiary-level tables which are for the entry of basic information. These are similar and wholly compatible with the secondary-level tables and are shown in use in the example given in Appendix III. When a separate model is used for estimating software development costs relevant data for some elements will be output by the model and can be entered directly into the secondary-level tables. In these circumstances some of the tertiary-level tables will not be required.

4.4   Assessment

The main elements under this item are effort and resources for the following:

- Justification.
- Technical feasibility including initial prototyping.
- Macro cost profile and cost—benefit assessment.

Many people would argue that assessment costs should not be included as part of software costs, but experience shows that either a lot of money is spent on studies that are out of all proportion to the software being considered, or major software developments are launched with little or no resources directed at the assessment. One consequence of the latter situation is that often no tangible measure of the potential benefit is established before a commitment is made.

Table 4.3 Value of investment in pre-project assessment

Item	Stock control system	Maintenance system	Accounting system
Assessment	300,000	200,000	10,000
Requirements design implementation, etc.	2,600,000	1,000,000	2,500,000
TIC	2,900,000	1,200,000	2,510,000
Benefit per year	£1,500,000	£2,000,000	None

Management will often make a commitment to a study team without too much thought as to the cost. Typically it goes like this: 'the accounting system seems to be creaking a bit these days — it's 10 years old now — perhaps we should set up a study team. It is important to the company as a whole so the team should be led by a Director.' This commitment is likely to cost about £100,000. This is soon followed by 'we have had a quick look — think we should get some consultants in to give us a hand'. This is likely to cost another £100,000. So £200,000 has been committed before any benefit has been even guesstimated. Despite the way in which action is sometimes initiated there is no question, though, that pre-project assessment is essential and is the only way in which the potential benefit of a system can be properly identified and quantified. The examples in Table 4.3 vividly illustrate the importance of adequate provision for assessment in the overall estimate for a software project.

There are two good reasons for including assessment costs in the TIC:

1. It is the *total* cost of the software project that should be set against the estimated benefit.
2. Experience shows, as illustrated in Table 4.3, that unless there is a reasonable budget allowance for assessment then the software could turn out to be a white elephant in terms of benefit.

Table 4.4 Total installed cost template — assessment

Primary cost elements	Elapsed time from start										Total
	1	2	3	4	5	6	7	8	9	10	
Justification: study team consultants											
Technical feasibility: study team consultants prototyping											
Macro estimating											
Cost–benefit assessment											
Assessment costs											

A spreadsheet for recording the assessment costs is given in Table 4.4. The timescale used in this spreadsheet, and in all those in following sections, should be consistent with that in Table 4.1 so that the summary line of each primary element table can be directly transferred to the cost profile template. This is of particular importance as it ensures easy updating to the cost estimates in the progression from macro level to detail.

4.5   Requirements definition

This will vary according to the options being considered:

- Custom development in-house.
- Custom development by systems house.
- Package solution.

The mix of second level elements will be some combination of the following:

- Preparation of functional specification.
- Review of functional specification.
- Infrastructure specification.
- Preparation of statement of requirements (SOR).
- Preparation of invitation to tender (ITT).
- Evaluation of responses to SOR or ITT.

The importance of these functions should not be underestimated — the allocation

Table 4.5 Total installed cost template — requirements definition

Primary cost elements	Elapsed time from start										Total
	1	2	3	4	5	6	7	8	9	10	
Preparation of functional specification											
Review of functional specification											
Infrastructure specification											
Preparation of statement of requirements											
Evaluation of statement of requirements											
Preparation of invitation to tender											
Evaluation of responses to invitation to tender											
Requirements definition costs											

of sufficient effort to these functions is vital to ensure that the project is established on a sound footing and the requirements and commitment are fully understood by all concerned. The importance of the ITT and the SOR is dealt with in more detail in Chapter 10.

A spreadsheet for requirements definition is given in Table 4.5

4.6 Software tools

It is essential to include in the estimate costs that may be incurred for third-party software required for the development of the proposed software system. Software tools fall into three categories:

1. Design and coding tools.
2. Project management and administration tools.
3. Project support tools.

Project support tools need particular mention. Although a word processing package will be required for general administration purposes there may in addition be a need for desktop publishing software for the preparation of documentation. Another major item may be a development licence for a DBMS and in particular a temporary licence for Systems House use for the duration of the development. It is always important to check on licensing arrangements as existing licences for third-party software may not cover the requirements of the proposed project.

The licence charges for software tools that need to be considered include the following:

* CASE tools.
* Languages.
* Development DBMS.
* Desktop publishing.
* Word processing.
* Project planning.
* Project accounting.
* Estimating models.

Although there may already be existing licences for the relevant tools, corporate policy often dictates that an appropriate proportion is cross charged or apportioned to all projects undertaken by the IT department.

A spreadsheet for software tools is given in Table 4.6.

4.7 Hardware facilities for development

There are two particular circumstances when hardware costs should be directly accounted for as part of a software development:

1. When additional hardware is required in order to provide facilities for the

Table 4.6 Total installed cost template — software tools

Primary cost elements	Elapsed time from start										Total
	1	2	3	4	5	6	7	8	9	10	
Design and coding tools: CASE tools languages development DBMS											
Project management and administration: word processing desktop publishing project planning project accounting estimating model											
Software tools costs											

development. This includes the communication links between the 'project' office and the system network.

2.   When specialist hardware is required for development and subsequent running of the system.

Hardware facilities directly associated with operational running of the system can be included in this section or as an addition to the TIC. Some users of this approach have adopted the TIC template for all IT projects including those which are predominantly hardware. The advantage is one of consistency across all project estimating.

A spreadsheet for hardware for development is given in Table 4.7 but this should be adapted to the needs of each organisation and be specific on the hardware included for a particular project.

Table 4.7 Total installed cost template — hardware for development

Primary cost elements	Elapsed time from start										Total
	1	2	3	4	5	6	7	8	9	10	
Specialist hardware for development											
Specialist hardware for operation											
Additional terminals for development											
Communications facilities for development											
Hardware for development costs											

4.8 Design

Design methods are becoming much more formal and definitive in approach and estimating should be geared directly to those methods. However, the estimates of cost and duration should be set out against definitive tasks so that accomplishment can be compatible with the project plan. Project control and project accounting can be recorded as accomplishment, with identified major and minor milestones against which to assess progress. A useful structure for estimating is the following:

- System specification/system prototyping.
- Detailed requirements specification.
- Architectural design.
- Module design and specification.
- Software design and specification.
- Specification of system tests.
- Design and specification of acceptance tests.
- Specification of documentation.
- Specification of data take-on/database transfer.

In the future there is likely to be increasing use made of prototyping in the place of written specification and there will be a consequent change in manpower effort and the elapsed timescale for some stages of the design process.

Also, with much more help and tutorial material being incorporated as on-line facilities it is essential to include manpower effort and timescale for the design of documentation as part of the overall design work.

As software engineering design becomes more formal then activities such as

Table 4.8 Total installed cost template — design

Primary cost elements	Elapsed time from start										Total
	1	2	3	4	5	6	7	8	9	10	
System specification											
System prototyping											
Detailed requirements specification											
Architectural design											
Module design and specification											
Software design and specification											
Specification of system tests											
Design and specification of acceptance tests											
Specification of documentation											
Specification of data transfer/take-on											
Design costs											

design review will need to be included and appropriate effort, timescale and cost estimated for that work.

A spreadsheet for design costing is given in Table 4.8. This will need to be adapted to suit the design method and the use of any estimating model.

4.9   Development

The development process will follow the design methodology and design structure and identifiable steps will include the following:

- Software coding and unit testing.
- Module testing.
- Subsystem linking and testing.
- System integration.
- System interface testing.
- User documentation and help testing.
- System documentation.

A spreadsheet for development costing is given in Table 4.9. This will need to be adapted to reflect project organisation and team structure. It will also need to reflect the format of output from any estimating model. However, both design and development cost estimates must be kept on a consistent timescale with the other primary elements.

Table 4.9   Total installed cost template — development

Primary cost elements	Elapsed time from start										Total
	1	2	3	4	5	6	7	8	9	10	
Software coding and unit testing											
Module testing											
Subsystem linking and testing											
System integration											
System interface testing											
On-line help testing											
User documentation											
System documentation											
Development costs											

4.10   Implementation

The commissioning of systems is now a well-defined process and can often be done in hours compared with the weeks of effort involved only 10 or 15 years ago. On the other hand, user acceptance has become a much more rigorous process and must be fully taken into account in estimating the effort and timescale for system implementation. User acceptance is often in two stages — to test that the functionality meets the specification and then to test that the system is operationally robust and acceptable. The elements that should be included in this section are as follows:

- Preparation and loading of acceptance test database.
- Installation and commissioning of operational hardware.
- Data clean-up and restructuring.
- Database loading.
- Manual data loading.
- Operational acceptance testing.
- Fault listing and rectification.
- Decommissioning existing system.

A spreadsheet for implementation costs is given in Table 4.10.

Table 4.10 Total installed cost template — implementation

Primary cost elements	Elapsed time from start										Total
	1	2	3	4	5	6	7	8	9	10	
Preparation and loading of acceptance test database											
Functional acceptance testing											
Stress testing											
Installation and commissioning											
Data clean-up and restructuring											
Database loading											
Manual data loading											
Operational acceptance testing											
Fault listing and fault rectification											
Decommissioning of existing system											
Implementation costs											

4.11 Training

Training, particularly of end users of the system, has an important bearing on achieving the benefit of the system and hence justifying the cost of developing the system. All too often provision of effort and time, for adequate training of the end users, is omitted and the full potential of the system is never achieved. In extreme cases the users default to 'private', manual or their own PC systems, and there is no net benefit from the new system even though it may have enormous

Table 4.11 Total installed cost template — training

Primary cost elements	Elapsed time from start										Total
	1	2	3	4	5	6	7	8	9	10	
Training of project team											
Design and loading of training database											
Preparation of training programme											
Training of operational support staff											
Training of help desk											
Training of users											
Training costs											

operational potential. The training elements that need to be costed include the following:

- Training of the project team in the use of the design and development tools.
- Design, preparation and loading of the system training database.
- Preparation of the training programme.
- Training of operational support staff, including help desk.
- Training of users.

A spreadsheet for training cost estimates is given in Table 4.11.

4.12   Project management and administration

Project management should begin at the justification stage and end when the post-project review is completed. In between these points there are a whole host of management and administrative activities that should be included to ensure the project is kept on course. The concept of a 'Project Office' is now more widely used in software engineering. Within that framework all administrative functions are dealt with and all resources are requisitioned. The Project Office services the project and must function from pre-project stage to post-project review.

The main elements that must be considered in this section in preparing an estimate include the following:

- Project management effort.
- Project administration effort.
- Administrative hardware and stationery.
- Accommodation at project site.
- Accommodation at remote sites.
- Travel costs and subsistence at remote sites.
- Quality assurance, quality control and audit effort.

Table 4.12 Total installed cost template — project management and administration

Primary cost elements	Elapsed time from start										Total
	1	2	3	4	5	6	7	8	9	10	
Project management											
Project administration											
Administrative hardware											
Administrative stationery											
Accommodation at project site											
Accommodation at remote site											
Travel and subsistence costs											
QA, QC and audit											
Cost estimating and project accounting											
Project planning and project control											
Staff recruiting costs											
Project management and administration costs											

- Cost estimating and project accounting.
- Project planning and project control.
- Staff recruiting costs.

A spreadsheet for project management and administration is given in Table 4.12.

4.13 Operational software

Very little, if any, applications software is now standalone. Software systems are dependent on one or a number of other packages which in the broad sense constitute the support environment. These are in most instances bought in, or third-party software, which for estimating purposes have a known price tag.

Operational software includes the following items:

- DBMS.
- Graphics.
- Systems security.
- Operating environment.

The initial licence fee (or proportion of that fee) for third-party software, required to support and run the proposed system, may, in some cases, be as much as 50% of the TIC and should be included in the estimate. A spreadsheet for operational software costs is given in Table 4.13.

Table 4.13 Total installed cost template — operational software

Primary cost elements	Elapsed time from start										Total
	1	2	3	4	5	6	7	8	9	10	
CAD package											
DBMS											
Graphics package											
System security software											
Operational environment											
Operational software costs											

4.14   Using the TIC approach

TIC is a template which should be used as a basis for estimating purposes. If it is to be of value then there are some basic rules that should be observed in using the TIC template.

1. The estimates may have to be prepared in a defined corporate format — this has the advantage of consistency in presentation and meets an important criterion for subsequent use, namely comparing like with like without having to modify or 'interpret' someone else's estimates. The primary and secondary estimating elements can be adapted to meet the needs of a particular organisation but:

    (a) cutting it down significantly, because 'a lot of it is not relevant to us', is dangerous in a changing environment and can lead to the omission of significant elements of cost;

    (b) adding to the list significantly will only make it more cumbersome and discourage people from going through the complete range of elements. In any case the 10 primary elements provide sufficient detail for appraisal by senior management and for comparative assessment purposes.

2. Where a software costing model is used the *relevant* primary elements of the TIC need to be related to that model output. However, most formal models will only cover part of the full cost covered in the foregoing and it is essential that the 'region of fit' is clearly established — see Cover (5).

    This is likely to be much easier and more reliability can be ensured when an analog or function point method is used for software estimating. However, with sufficient attention in the set-up process it is possible to ensure that 'double counting' or 'omission' is avoided when the TIC template is used in conjunction with an algorithmic model.

3. Once a basis for a TIC template has been established, that template must be used consistently at all levels of the organisation and for all purposes.

Senior management will welcome receiving costings that are in a consistent form and from which they can readily see the main elements of cost. This is particularly useful when options are being examined or where initial estimates have been refined in step with detailed design — such estimates have enhanced credibility.

4. Presenting what purports to be a TIC without a breakdown is *unacceptable*. The purpose of the primary element breakdown is to indicate that *all* aspects of software cost have been covered, and management are not going to get any eleventh-hour surprises because inexperienced people have omitted a major cost item.

4.15   Adaptability to changing needs

Software costing models that focus on estimates related primarily to the software coding aspects will contribute less to TIC in the future and indeed the relevance of 'lines of code' as an indicator of effort and cost to get a system operational is diminishing rapidly. In 1988 Cover (5) identified a number of important factors that will pose a challenge to software cost estimation in the future. A modified, and updated, view on that is summarised below:

1. The advent of fourth- and fifth-generation languages.
2. The emergence of standard software modules for activities such as data handling and user security.
3. The emergence of the strategic software environment (SSE) where data management and database handling is separated from user software.
4. Advanced CASE tools which automate specification techniques.
5. Advances in the hardware environment that aid programming.
6. Wider use of expert system shells and techniques.

This is not exhaustive — who knows what will emerge in the next decade — but it does vividly indicate the need for adaptability in the way software development is estimated and costed.

The TIC template is not a solution that will give a good or bad estimate — it is an approach, a method that is flexible and usable in a variety of situations. The output, the total installed cost, is an estimate that is only as good as the individual estimates derived for the elements. However, its particular strength is that everything that is likely to contribute to the cost of getting a software system operational can be accounted for and included.

4.16   An illustration of TIC in practice

The TIC approach has been used successfully on a range of projects. Table 4.14 is a summary of the estimates prepared at the various stages for a custom-developed stock control system. The table gives the initial macro estimate together with pre-specification and post-specification estimates and a final post-project cost. This

Table 4.14 Comparison of TIC from macro estimate to post-project review

Primary cost element	Macro estimate	Pre-specification	Post-specification	Post-project
Assessment	300,000	300,000	300,000	300,000
Requirements definition	50,000	110,000	110,000	114,000
Software tools	10,000	50,000	45,000	48,000
H/W facilities	50,000	50,000	55,000	55,000
Design		350,000	450,000	460,000
Development	200,000	775,000	700,000	750,000
Implementation		460,000	550,000	540,000
Training	150,000	150,000	150,000	180,000
Project management and administration	50,000	245,000	250,000	250,000
Operational software	240,000	195,000	200,000	240,000
TIC	£1,050,000	£2,685,000	£2,810,000	£2,937,000

has been found to be an ideal way to present information to management. The macroestimate was prepared using the analog model discussed in Appendix II and the detail for this example is given in Appendix III. The preparation of the pre-specification estimate is also given in Appendix III.

Table 4.15 is a comparison of costed options for the replacement of a maintenance management system. Four options have been costed at macro level and each shows a broad breakdown. The options considered were: continuing to use the existing operational package, enhancing the existing package, specification and development of a new custom system, or customising an off-the-shelf package. The last option was chosen and a more detailed breakdown of the costs is given in Tables 6.2 to 6.10. As in the case above these estimates were prepared using the spreadsheets in the same way as indicated in Appendix III for the previous example. Both of the above examples are based on actual software projects.

4.17   Need for TIC approach

Much more attention in the software industry is now being focused on standards and quality, led by professional organisations such as the British Computer Society (BCS) and the Institute of Electrical and Electronics Engineers (IEEE) as well as the various standards bodies. There is also growing interest in quality as a corporate objective based on total quality management (TQM) principles. The UK Department of Trade and Industry Tick IT scheme was initiated in 1990 to promote the concept of quality management systems (QMS) directed specifically at IT but working within the context of TQM. The TQM improvement model put forward had three elements:

Table 4.15 Comparison of TIC macro estimate for system replacement options

Primary cost element	Support existing package	Enhance existing package	Specify and develop new system	Customise off-the- shelf system
Assessment*	200,000	200,000	200,000	200,000
Requirements definition	10,000	90,000	230,000	150,000
Software tools	0	50,000	100,000	0
H/W facilities for development	0	0	50,000	0
Design	20,000	100,000	450,000	40,000
Development	60,000	120,000	600,000	80,000
Implementation	5,000	80,000	200,000	200,000
Training	0	0	150,000	180,000
Project management and administration	5,000	40,000	150,000	100,000
Operational software	70,000	70,000	70,000	250,000
TIC	£370,000	£750,000	£2,200,000	£1,200,000

* Whatever option is selected the full assessment cost must be included

1. Management commitment to improve.
2. Motivation to improve.
3. Measurement for improvement.

The total installed cost (TIC) template discussed in the foregoing is needed as a base for improved costing of software projects and fits into the context of these TQM elements in the following way:

Management commitment to improve

Senior management in most organisations are seeking ways to improve the costing of software and would welcome an approach that provides a consistent format for the presentation and assessment of projects. Being able to see at a glance how the various options compare and to see successive changes for a project on a comparative basis are of immense value to decision makers.

Motivation to improve

This is always greatly enhanced if there is a basis on which software cost estimates can be set out and understood at all levels in the organisation. The consistent approach set out in the TIC template ensures that all types of software cost estimates are presented in the same format and all levels of the organisation are using the same figures. A consistent approach aids motivation as has been apparent from the projects already costed using this format.

Measurement for improvement

The TIC template can be used from the conceptual stage of a project through to the post-project review as illustrated in Table 4.14. Furthermore this approach makes it possible to see the project as a whole, at any stage of the overall process, and where post-project review feeds back to the estimating process it provides a consistent format that aids data collection and presentation. This is therefore a sound basis for good measurement and leads on to improvement in the whole process of software costing.

5 Linking estimating and project planning

5.1 Links between planning and cost estimating

This book is about cost estimating but there is such a close affinity with project planning that the two aspects of setting up a sound basis for a project must be considered as interwoven. In many projects cost and resource estimates are prepared separately from project schedules and this leads to an immediate inconsistency even before the project has been started. One reason is that there is a philosophical difference of approach between estimators and planners. Estimators think in terms of things — resource by quantity — whilst planners think in terms of actions — using resources to accomplish tasks. The other important factor in relation to software in particular is that estimating is not yet established as a skill base within software engineering, so there is no professional focus for planners to establish a basis of common policy and interchange of ideas. This must change because only with the combined skills of estimating and planning will it be possible for the software industry to build a good foundation for future projects. Wright (18), writing on IT and organisational change, said 'Software Houses have increasingly to deliver against a fixed price, not an estimate and an open cheque book. Some of them are in trouble because they cannot change their own way of working.' This is a sweeping generalisation but there are still too many instances when it is true. However, this is not a matter that is confined to software houses; it is equally true of many projects undertaken by in-house IT departments.

A good system design is wasted technical effort unless it can be funded, based on sound estimates, and accomplished, based on a realistic plan.

It is essential therefore that design, estimating and planning are carried out as complementary activities, as illustrated in Figure 5.1, and furthermore that there is a one-to-one correspondence between the structure, the main tasks and the milestones. There are two important reasons for this:

1. It may be necessary to revise the plan and estimate in the light of technical evaluation of part of the system, such as the outcome of prototyping, and it is then necessary to make revisions to the relevant parts of the plan and cost estimate, directly and efficiently, to give a revised built-up cost and a revised schedule.
2. The final estimate will become the project budget which, together with the plan, will be the basis on which management will commit to the project.

Figure 5.1
Estimator's view of
project

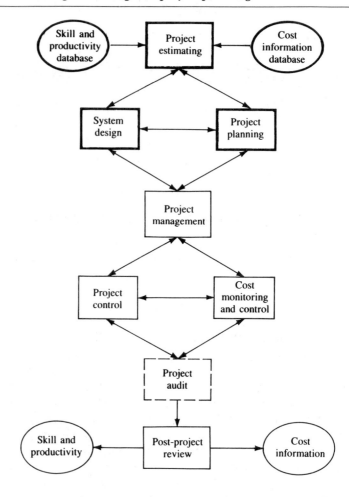

Reporting progress against the plan, and costs against the budget, should follow as a matter of course and these should relate directly to the accomplishment of milestones in the development of the system.

The inescapable conclusion from this is that cost estimating and cost control must be closely linked. At all stages of software costing there must be commitment to the use of accurate information that is wholly compatible with that used for planning.

5.2   Project schedule and cash flow

The project plan should be a detailed statement of how the software development will be undertaken, covering the following:

- The timescale of phases to completion.
- The resources to be used and at what rate over the timescale.
- The review and decision points.
- Milestones in the development.

It is not until a project plan has been drafted that the timescale for the use of the resources can be established and this leads on to a cost schedule defined as a cost profile. Two things are of particular interest to senior management at this stage:

1. When is the money required over the timescale of the project?
2. When, in the timescale of the project, will there be something deliverable or even usable?

Answers on these matters may well influence the decision to commit to the project as proposed. In some instances there may be a call for revision to the design structure and the project schedule so that there is an improved cash flow and consequent reduction in financial risk. In all good project plans there should be milestones, as early as practical in the schedule, that are related to deliverables, so that there is a tangible return on the investment so far before more money is committed to the next stage.

With the advent of CASE tools has come the facility to have interfaces between the structured systems design and project planning facilities. It is not an automatic process — it requires intelligent use, and remember that the A in CASE is for Aided! However, the next step is to build an effective bridge from design and planning to estimating.

5.3   Integration of estimating and planning data

The majority of planning packages have been developed for general use and are not specific to software engineering. On the other hand the cost estimation models discussed in Chapter 3 are specific to software development and some provide a facility for estimating timescales as well as manpower effort. This limited scheduling facility is focused on the software code aspects and is not a satisfactory basis for developing a full plan covering all aspects of the project. There is therefore a need for a general project planning facility to be used for all software development work. There is no evidence to suggest that the costing models, discussed in Chapter 3, have been interfaced to general project planning systems but there should be no major difficulty in arranging output from a model to be exported to a planning system.

There are various ways in which estimating and planning facilities can be arranged so that data interchange can be organised. Westney (19) carried out a review of the possible approaches and the following is a digest of the seven possible approaches to the integration of estimating and planning.

1. Use design information to generate both planning and estimating data simultaneously

This has been done successfully in some areas of heavy engineering using, for example, the Icarus package, but no package exists in the software industry at present.

2. Provide an estimating database applications-writing capability

This requires a proprietary language and database suitable for writing estimating programs that can interface and exchange data with a planning package. Examples cited are dBase interfacing with Open Plan and Artemis.

3. Use the planning software as a method for estimating

This requires a flexible coding and reporting facility in the planning package. This is often used in engineering projects where there is a well-established pattern of working and there is no complex content to the project. It is an approach that is unlikely to provide a satisfactory basis for estimating and planning software development in the short term.

4. Export the information from planning software to general-purpose software

This is useful as a supplement to approach 3 above so that indirect and other costs can be added to the direct costs generated by the planning package. Examples quoted are Harvard Project Manager and Superproject Expert exporting to Lotus, but as mentioned in approach 3 it has little relevance to software costing methods.

5. Integrate estimating data with a scheduling algorithm in the same program

This, like approach 1 above, is useful in some engineering situations and an example quoted is the Star Watch package where a predefined, highly integrated structure for design, costing and planning can be used. This is not the same as having the three functions as complementary activities discussed in Section 5.1. It may be possible at some time in the future to adopt this approach but it is not currently relevant to effective software costing.

6. Provide a flexible user-defined estimating program with export capabilities to planning and scheduling software

This is a good approach where no formal estimating procedures are in place and an analog model for estimating is being set up. This can be set up as a user-defined spreadsheet designed to export to an appropriate planning package.

7. Provide an interface between estimating and planning software

This is the approach that will enable the most suitable systems to be used for each of the stages in setting up a successful project. The opportunity should always be taken to establish that the facilities provided in an estimating system and a planning system are wholly suited to the project environment before going to the expense of an interface. Do not just follow what someone else has done, nor is it advisable to interface an existing planning package with a new costing model without a careful review of needs on the one hand and package facilities on the other.

Whatever approach is taken it must always be borne in mind that the flow of data between design, estimating and planning is not one way or one off. The process of establishing a sound basis for a viable project is one of iteration within each aspect and a trade-off between the three aspects. There is a need to ensure that the identifiable elements of system structure — modularity and constructability — are wholly compatible with the input to estimating and planning and vice versa so that iteration can be carried out easily and consistently.

5.4 Review of the plan

In Chapter 3 mention was made of the need to introduce design review as an activity that should be identified and carried out and that the effort for this should be included in the estimates. There is also a need to carry out a review of the project plan — planning packages are methods not solutions — with the aim of ensuring that the plan is robust and complete.

The three main objectives in preparing a project plan are as follows:

1. To include every task and activity.
2. To allow sufficient time for each task to be completed.
3. To schedule the tasks in a logical order and over an elapsed time that allows resources to be used in an effective manner.

Unless these basic requirements are met then it may well be that it is impractical to carry out the project to the proposed plan and the cost estimate will be invalid. Experience indicates that costs will increase by *at least 25%* if an unrealistic project plan is prepared.

A useful basis for review, which should be independent of the planning package facilities, is to use a checklist. Methods and tools may change but the overall requirement remains the same — thoroughness. A good foundation for the review of the design, plan and estimate is 'How to install successful computer systems' developed by SD-Scicon and reproduced in Appendix IV.

Finally it is worth reminding ourselves that the project plan is the basic source of information for project control and is intimately linked to cost control. Each time an activity or task is changed in the project plan a corresponding change should be made to the cost estimate, and unless the change is very minor in nature there may well be a knock-on effect to the cash flow and so a check should always be made on that part of the costing.

5.5   Timescales

It seems to be a fact of life that some people earnestly believe that setting, and demanding, unrealistic timescales has some merit. Those who do not or will not resist such demands, and allow themselves to be forced into producing schedules to unrealistic dates, are heading for trouble before the project has even started.

The optimum manpower loading determines the realistic timescale for completion of a software module. The schedule of modules in the overall plan is determined by the system design structure and the interaction between the modules. The linking and testing of modules must be done in a logical way that reflects the way in which they will function together. Shortening the overall timescale by scheduling modules in an unrealistic way will only lead to system conflicts and make it necessary to backtrack, reschedule and almost certainly overrun the original timetable.

Beware of those who ask today for something tomorrow — they should be asked why they did not action the matter in good time and if they can really afford the risk and high cost involved in working to an unrealistic timescale.

Three things determine the overall timescale for a project:

1. Pre-project work — design, estimating and planning.
2. Mobilisation to start the work, including approvals, sanctions and contracts.
3. Completion of the project activities up to the point of handover for operational use.

Setting a target date for completion has no relevance unless it is based on a knowledge of the likely duration of the project and the reality of mobilising to start the project by the appropriate date. There are no shortcuts to setting up a project — if any are taken it is usually necessary to revise the schedule with a corresponding *increase* in the project costs.

6 Preparing the cost estimate

6.1 Approach to estimating

The key question at the start of the estimating process is the scope of the estimate relative to the TIC, for example:

* What is the estimate required to cover?
* What quality of estimate is required?
* How firm is the estimate?

It will be assumed here that an assessment has been done and there is agreement to proceed further with the project, subject to an acceptable design, development plan and estimate of cost. There are two approaches that can be followed:

1. An estimate can be prepared for the *whole* project but as this is prior to the requirements definition and any firm specification and schedule, it will be based on assumptions that may not be valid at a later stage.

   This estimate can only be regarded as a budgetary estimate and will be subject to variation by at least 50%.

   Experience shows that this same level of estimating error applies even for the purchase of an off-the-shelf package if it is prepared prior to the requirements definition.

   Although this is the traditional approach and is still used by many organisations it has an underlying weakness that will be reflected in one of the following ways:

   (a) The estimate will have to be revised in the light of a requirements definition and an agreed specification, so in reality the estimate is no advance on the broad-based macro estimate discussed in Chapter 2. Estimates of this kind, presented to management and then repeatedly revised upwards, only confirm to senior management that IT staff have little or no grasp of commercial reality.

   (b) The estimate will be loaded with contingency — wild guesstimates that may or may not cover the costs of the system defined later in the requirements definition. One outcome of this approach, if the estimated cost becomes the project budget, is that the design will have to be tailored to the budget *not* the requirement.

2. An estimate can be prepared for the requirements definition stage only and

the output from that work will not only define how the software needs can best be met but also provide a basis for a firm estimate for the subsequent stages of the project.

This is an approach being increasingly used for all types of work and all sizes of project. Some far-sighted organisations are now putting the requirements definition out to tender with the resulting benefit of two or three well-thought-through solutions to the software requirement together with project plans and cost estimates for the design and development stages. This is new thinking and involves a higher initial cost — paying for more than one requirements definition — but the overall benefit is a well-considered design and a much more stable estimate for the ensuing project.

If the software industry is to improve the reliability of cost estimating then it must become standard practice to carry out the requirements definition as a standalone stage, following on from the assessment, and preceding any commitment to the development. The outcome from the requirements definition would then be used as the basis for costing the development.

6.2   Basis of the proposed system

One of the major issues that can only be properly identified at the requirements definition stage is the basis for the proposed system. This could be one of the following:

- An off-the-shelf package solution.
- An off-the-shelf package solution with enhancements.
- A core system with major customisation.
- A custom-designed system.

In some situations other options may be considered and possibly adopted which include the following:

- Turning a previous custom system development into a core system or package.
- Taking an existing specification and design and developing the system for a different operational environment from the original or rewriting in, say, a 4GL.

This is not an exhaustive list of the possible optional ways in which a new software requirement can be satisfied.

A clear distinction needs to be made here when referring to any form of existing software in this context. It is a question of selecting and actually using existing software for the construction of the new system, as discussed in Sections 2.5 and 2.7. It is not a matter of using previous software development effort as a basis for estimating as discussed in Appendix II. Where modules of software can be reused in their entirety in a new system there is a known cost and estimating of effort is not required.

There is the added bonus from modules and components of reusable software in that they are proven in operational use and some reduction in system testing may be possible. However, a certain amount of caution is necessary — whilst the module may functionally match what is required, checks should be made to ensure that it can be used in the context of the structure, linkage and interaction with other parts of the proposed software environment.

6.3   System infrastructure

In the past many systems were developed as stand alones working within the confines of one operational environment. The requirement now is for systems to form an integrated operational support facility for meeting user needs whether in the technical, administrative and commercial aspects of the business.

The system infrastructure requirements must be specified as part of the requirements definition. The effort and cost involved in providing data and systems links and interfaces must be estimated and included as part of the system costs. These costs are not insignificant and in some cases can amount to as much as 25% of the TIC.

Ignoring the system infrastructure is likely to lead to untold problems and trying to 'force-fit' a system retrospectively into an operational environment will be a very expensive business.

Another aspect of the system infrastructure which must be taken into account is required portability of the proposed software. Portability is a much abused word. Sometimes it is used to describe transferability — where *versions* of the same software can be used on a range of hardware. Also some organisations now look for applications software that is 'compatible' up or down a range of one manufacturer's hardware, i.e. all users have the same system but users in different locations may be running it on anything from a PC to a mainframe computer.

For the purposes of consistency portability should be regarded as software that can be moved between hardware systems without the need for change. We are now able to achieve portability with an operating system like UNIX, and its derivatives, combined with DBMS and SQL facilities that are independent of hardware.

The question that has to be addressed in cost estimating for a portable system is which parts of the software infrastructure are to be included in the project cost. The choice is likely to be some combination of the following:

*   Operating system.
*   Software language.
*   DBMS.
*   Applications system.

6.4   Third-party software and services

In the foregoing and in Chapter 3 there is reference to third-party software that is required for either development of the system (software tools etc.) or operation of the system (DBMS etc.)

The licence cost for both types of software must be included in the estimate for the proposed system, either as a full cost or as a proportion of total cost where it is corporate policy to spread the third-party facility charges across relevant applications systems. However, it must never be assumed that because an organisation has a licence for Product X that the licence allows unlimited use. Checks must be made on any existing arrangements to determine whether licence restrictions apply such as the following:

- It is specific to a particular hardware configuration.
- There is a limit on the number of users.
- It is for run-time use only.

The cost of extended use must be established and included in the relevant part of the TIC template. It is always a wise precaution to ask the potential supplier to give a quotation which clearly sets out what is being provided, on what basis and in what quantity. At this stage there will be no contractual commitment with a third-party supplier but it is important to establish clearly what the quotation covers and get specific information on the following:

- Initial licence charge.
- Annual licence charge and from when it applies.
- Installation charges.
- Cost of help line and support.
- User manuals.
- In which country and currency the price is fixed.

Where the project involves the use of an unfamiliar third-party package, allowance must be made for the initial training of project staff and also for the training of operational support staff.

It may also be desirable to establish a core skill base for the proposed project by drawing upon staff from either the package supplier or a software house. The cost of that manpower must be included in the estimate. For the cost of these staff services it is necessary to establish the following:

- The standard day rate and whether this is an all-inclusive rate at the project site.
- The applicability of the standard rate and any variation to that rate for additional time outside the normal working day.
- Additional charges for staff working away from the project site.

One final point on third-party quotations for use in an estimate: it is essential to establish the validity period of the quote in relation to the decision timescale for project budget approval, mobilisation of the team and the call-off of third-party resources.

6.5 Skill assessment and productivity

The software industry is influenced by some particular manpower trends that can have a profound influence on the cost estimating of software:

1. Staff are highly mobile and change jobs more frequently than in most other sectors of the economy.
2. Staff expect to advance rapidly and working skill, vested in individuals, is lost as these individuals progress into management.
3. People entering the software industry are highly motivated and learn quickly.
4. Techniques, methods and tools change very frequently.
5. Large projects may be staffed by a mixed team drawn from in-house and software houses.

The main factors that affect productivity within the project environment are only partly related to the skill of the team members. In practice the following have been found to be of particular importance:

• The size of the staff skill base available.
• Manpower loading on the project.
• Staff turnover.
• System design.
• Project management.

On projects of short duration with a short and certain mobilisation period, it is often possible to identify individuals from the available skill base who will constitute the working team. However, for projects of longer duration, or where the start date is some way off, this is not usually possible. The judgement then has to centre on the general level of relevant skill, the need to supplement this with training to add to the pool and the expected demands on the skill base over the duration of the project from all sources. Indeed, it is not recommended that project estimates or schedules are based on the skill of any particular individuals, as this can easily result in exposure and underestimating if staff of less experience have to be used when the project starts. The main consideration is that skill levels and productivity of staff may vary from project to project and it is important to assess skill in an objective way. Insufficient attention is given to this matter and the assessment and reassessment of individual skill in relation to learning curves is not often done. On projects of short duration the skill level at the outset is crucial. On the other hand, projects lasting 6 months and longer will have not only a slower build-up of the team but also of the skill level of individuals; the team as a whole will increase as the project progresses and overall productivity will often be satisfactory even if the overall starting level is below average.

Staff turnover may have an adverse effect on projects of long duration if skilled members of the team are lost to the project due to promotion, job changing, etc. Even if one makes the assumption that an equally skilled person will be available for substitution some allowance must be made in the estimated effort and timescale for a period of familiarisation and settling down with the team. This is dealt with in more detail in Section 7.3. Any change in staffing will affect productivity to some degree and some allowance should be made in the estimate for what is judged to be an appropriate level of attrition.

Productivity, individually and overall, will be influenced more by team organisation and leadership than by individual levels of skill. Manpower loading and organisation are crucial factors and an optimum balance must be sought which aims at maximising productivity overall. Overloading is in some ways worse than a shortfall in skilled staff. For every project there is an optimum manpower loading which should be identified and used as the basis for the schedule and estimate. The key to identifying that optimum is the design structure and the organisation of the teams to undertake the packages of work relevant to that structure. Putnam and Fitzsimmons (20) have set some useful guidelines, but with a rapidly changing approach to software design and development based on structured methods and using CASE tools these will need modification. However, the general principles continue to apply to team structures within the framework of the project environment.

Productivity on a project is a complex function involving the way in which effort, time and technology are combined. The choice of software language, screen handler, DBMS, etc. can, in some instances, have more influence on productivity for a particular development than the skill of the individual team members. If the tools and the software environment do not match the proposed system then project staff will not achieve their expected productivity irrespective of their individual skill level. The other factor that has a profound influence is the design structure; in particular it must be possible to construct the modules separately and then to link them into the system structure. In the event this is a matter of the teams working initially on parts of the system and then interacting as the work progresses. The skills and the productivity of the teams must be balanced in a way that enables the process of construction to proceed in an orderly way without waste of effort and without periods of enforced idleness.

The project environment is a working environment with interactions up and down the organisational structure and between the team members and the project manager. Of the total time team members spend on the project, only a relatively small proportion is focused directly on the technical product. A significant amount of time is taken up in indirect activities such as job communication, referring to manuals, contributing to progress reports, reviewing work schedules, etc. An analysis made by Boehm (11) suggests that programmers only spend some 13% of their time writing programs. The overall level of productivity of any project is very much geared to the project environment and the cohesion of the team. A highly motivated team will produce more work of better quality than a team of low morale. Again, as in the other points mentioned above, this is irrespective of the skill and experience of the team members. The degree of motivation achieved over the duration of the project will be significantly influenced by the project manager, particularly the amount of management effort that is directed at the mobilisation of resources and effort, encouraging and helping with the solution of problems and by ensuring that the overall working conditions for the team are satisfactory. The estimator, however, should also consider the likely conditions under which the team will be working and include any appropriate allowance in the estimates for unusual or difficult features of the prospective project environment. This is a matter that should not be ignored, nor should the influence on the project be underestimated. DeMarco and Lister (16) suggest that 'human reactions are complicated and never very crisp and clean in their effects, but they matter more than any other aspect of the work'.

6.6 Basis of the project

Estimates are made by those involved with doing the work for submission to those who require the end product and control a budget. The 'buyer' may be an internal department, another part of the corporate group, or a third party.

The person or organisation preparing the estimate must establish the basis on which the project is to be carried out. The items to be covered include the following:

- Who is providing accommodation and support facilities for the team and on what basis?
- What hardware resources are required and how, where and when will they be made available?
- Who is meeting the cost of the hardware resources?
- What are the time constraints and cost consequences of delay or variation in the provision of support facilities?
- What review points and approvals are required?
- Are the timescales for starting and finishing realistic, can the project team and resources be mobilised in time and what are the consequences of a delayed start?
- What acceptance procedures and warranty procedures are required?
- What is the proposed payment profile, retentions, etc.?

The cost estimate for a software project is a crucial part of the information on which the vendor is undertaking the work and on which the buyer is committing to the purchase of the system. This may range in value from a few thousand to tens of millions of pounds. There are enough risks and uncertainties involved without adding misunderstanding regarding the basis on which the project is to be conducted. The risks can be reduced by taking these matters fully into account when the estimate is prepared.

6.7 Inflation and exchange rates

Inflation is a fact of life and must be taken into account in appropriate parts of the project cost estimate. Furthermore the software industry is international and pricing structure will always be influenced by currency exchange rates, particularly for third-party software. Some of the ways in which inflation and the variation in exchange rates will influence software development projects are indicated in the following.

Staff effort for all aspects of a project — whether technical, administrative or management — should be estimated in man days, weeks or months. The effort should be distributed across the timescale of the project in line with the project

Table 6.1 Application of inflation over duration of project

Year	0	1	2	3	4	Total
Estimated inflation factor	1.0	1.07	1.18	1.26	1.36	—
Unit rate for software engineer	£300	£321	£354	£378	£408	—
Estimated effort in man weeks	0	800	3,000	3,000	2,000	8,800
Estimated cost	0	£256,000	£1,062,000	£1,134,000	£816,000	£3,268,000

plan to give a year-by-year distribution. This will enable appropriate rates to be applied to the proportions of the effort in each year. This is illustrated in Table 6.1 for a project that is expected to start in the fiscal year following that in which the estimate is being prepared, and then to run for a 4 year period. Taking full account of the effects of inflation gives an estimate of £3,268,000 compared with an estimate based solely on current staff costs of £2,640,000. The approach set out in Table 6.1 has the advantage that it can be used as follows:

- As soon as data is available on staff effort over the timescale of the project.
- For subsequent iterations of the estimate where effort, unit rate and inflation can be varied separately year on year.
- For project review to compile useful data for future estimating purposes.

It follows from the foregoing that allowance for forward cost increases must be applied to projects which are expected to go beyond the current fiscal year. Most organisations increase prices annually but not all conveniently on 1 January. Third-party cost increases must be assessed, whether they are for software packages (language compiler, DBMS, CASE) or staff resources or other services. The supplier may be willing to provide information but failing that an appropriate allowance for inflation should be included on a similar basis to that used for staff estimates in Table 6.1.

Exchange rates may need to be considered in relation to specific parts of the project estimate. Particular requirements include the following:

- Third-party software from another country needed for the project.
- Software modules developed abroad and charged for in a foreign currency.
- Staff working abroad during the development or installation.
- Staff from more than one country working on the project.

Wherever there is an overseas factor in a project then the implications of exchange rates on the project cost estimate must be looked at and taken into account. For projects of more than 6 months' duration allowance must be made for variation in the exchange rate and it is advisable to take a pessimistic view of trends.

The application of exchange rates to cost estimates is often a matter of corporate policy and not something that individuals should apply without consultation with and the formal agreement of senior management.

There are of course situations where the whole project is being done for an overseas organisation, in which case agreement has to be reached on the contractual currency of the project. In the preparation of the quotation an appropriate allowance for exchange rates must be applied to the whole cost of the project. It is often advisable to insist on the quotation and payment being in the currency of the contractor's home country but this may only be feasible if that is where the major part of the work is to be carried out. The advent of the European ECU will help in providing a more stable base for trading within Europe and it is to be hoped that it can also be used between Europe and North America.

In summary, what can be said without question is that careful consideration must be given to the whole matter of inflation and exchange rates and the relevance of each to the individual elements of the software development project, as well as the project as a whole.

6.8   Assumptions, unknowns and contingency

Even with the best will in the world one will be faced with situations where there may be some aspects of a project for which there is no information, or experience, on which to base an estimate. Where an item is an unknown quantity it should be identified as such and the basis on which estimating assumptions have been made should be set down. If this simple procedure is adopted then revision and reassessment can be done with more confidence. It is important to keep firmly in mind that the process is *estimating* and as such can be improved by a second or third pass and by input from other people and sources.

Contingency must be considered in its proper context. It is not a 'catch all' that can be used to cover unknown or doubtful aspects of a project. Too often it is used by the lazy and inept as an alternative to a clear and detailed evaluation of the work content of a job. It is used by management when they have serious reservations about the estimates presented for their approval. In many instances the estimated cost of software consists of a poor or superficial estimate with contingency piled upon contingency in a desperate hope that all unforeseen costs have been covered. The weakness of this approach should be self-evident:

- It is guessing, not estimating.
- If there is such uncertainty about the cost should there not be corresponding uncertainty about the effort, productivity and timescale?

Applying contingency in situations where technical innovation is involved can be very dangerous, particularly if the innovation applies widely in the software or where the new technique is likely to have a significant impact on system functionality. Innovative projects should be treated as research using prototyping and piloting. Stanley (22) contends that both history and logic suggest that cost overruns are endemic to innovative engineering.

DeMarco (3) considers that overruns on projects are very often due to insufficient information for estimating, insufficient understanding of the intricacies of the development environment, failure to consider the *true* complexity of the application and a consequent lack of contingency planning. Contingency should be used in estimating with the utmost caution and in relation to a few specific items in any particular project. The best way to proceed is to examine the specific item in an objective way, identify an alternative, less risky technique, and adopt this as a fallback option. Both the chosen solution and the fallback option should be costed and the elapsed time for completion of the task estimated. The two estimates should be added together and used as the time and cost estimate for that part of the project. However, this amounts in practice to adding a task or activity that can be estimated with some accuracy but which in the event may not be undertaken. The logic of this approach is that if, after effort and money has been expended on the chosen solution, it fails then there is a realistic *contingency* remaining in the budget for the fallback option to be undertaken. Furthermore there is also sufficient time in the plan for the fallback option to be carried out without an overrun on the planned schedule. This approach should be limited to particular aspects of the project which cannot be explored in other ways and viability established by prototyping or other means. To assume therefore that contingency has a role outside of small discrete parts of projects is quite misleading and can only lead to a continuation of the situation when many projects continue to overrun on budget due to lack of objective effort in planning and estimating.

6.9   Preparing the estimate

The objectives in estimating are as follows:

- To prepare an estimate of the total cost for getting a software system operational, be it a custom development or an off-the-shelf package.
- To assess the timescale over which the work can be accomplished and to prepare a corresponding cost profile.
- For projects that extend over more than one fiscal year prepare, from the cost profile, annual budget requirements as sub-budgets of the project.
- Assess the benefits from the use of the system and the timescale over which those can be achieved. The basic information should have been prepared at the assessment stage of the project.
- Combine the cost and benefit profiles and produce a cash flow profile.

In the foregoing some of the matters that need to be considered in cost estimating have been identified. In earlier chapters the basis of estimating has been set out. The task now is to prepare the detailed estimate for a proposed software system. The aim is to arrive at an estimate that is *complete*, covering all items for which a cost will be incurred and is *realistic*, representing the true cost of getting the software operational. The estimate of the total installed cost (TIC) cannot be derived from a model — as indicated in Chapter 4 the TIC is the accumulation of best estimates from a number of sources, including output from formal estimating models. It is essential that the TIC is realistic as it will form the basis for any adjustment considered necessary. This is discussed further in Section 6.10.

The process of preparing a TIC estimate requires a disciplined approach, the object of which is to make sure that everything relevant to the particular project is identified, costed and included in the built-up estimate. A series of 17 steps are set out in the following which are intended as a framework for covering all the relevant items. After step 8 they can be scheduled in any appropriate order, according to the expected duration of each step, so that there is convergence of all the information by the date the estimate has to be prepared.

Step 1 — Review requirements definition. This should cover the functional specification and infrastructure specification and is the detailed definition of user requirements and the operational environment in which the system will function.

Step 2 — Confirm the basis of the system. Is a package solution preferred to custom development or is it optional?

Step 3 — Confirm the system infrastructure. Have the operating system and DBMS been defined or are they optional? What is the user population and distribution? What are the performance criteria for the system?

Step 4 — Innovative feature. Are there any innovative features that need special attention — prototyping — or special development skills in the team?

Step 5 — Prototyping v. specification. Identify whether prototyping is an acceptable alternative to the specification of user facilities.

Step 6 — Set out TIC. The TIC template should be established and:

(a) assessment costs and global estimates, prepared in the feasibility study, should be entered;

(b) any items not relevant — secondary elements — should be identified;

(c) any special items not normally included in the secondary-level elements should be identified;

(d) the tertiary-level tables should be set up.

Step 7 — Identify the sources of the element estimates. The estimates for the main elements of the TIC are likely to come from more than one source. This will depend on how much of the project will be carried out in-house and how much will be contracted out. The possible sources of cost estimates include:

(a) the output from one or more estimating models, such as those discussed in Chapter 3 — it is essential to know the models being used and the 'region of fit' over the scope of the TIC elements;

(b) quotations from third parties for software tools, support software or staff effort — the scope of the quotation needs to be established as it may cover things like 'Project Management', 'Installation and Training' but there may also be in-house resources and costs to be included for these items;

(c) in-house costs for software or services to be charged to the project;

(d) costs associated with lost or reduced production in the particular operational area during the transfer of data files.

Step 8 — Prepare estimating schedule. This is the estimating plan, not the project plan, and is particularly important in preparing estimates for large projects. A simple plan or bar chart should be prepared which indicates the main activities involved in **preparing the estimate** — it is particularly important to allow sufficient time for the preparation of estimates by potential contractors or suppliers and for the subsequent aggregation of estimates from all sources (see Chapter 9).

Step 9 — Initiate estimates/quotes. The next action is to initiate the preparation of estimates and quotations from the various sources identified in step 7. It is of course important to ensure that the output required from external sources is clearly indicated so that adequate, accurate input information for the TIC is provided. In particular the format required for the following should be clearly indicated:

(a) initial licence plus annual licence for software packages;

(b) skills, numbers, duration and day rate for contract staff;

(c) TIC elements to be covered or excluded for contracted-out development.

This is discussed further in Chapter 9. The estimation process may also involve the use of a model for the software development part of the project. The key requirements in using the model are:

(a) that there is an adequate database for the input parameters;

(b) that care is taken in the selection of accurate cost driver ratings;

(c) that no personal judgement is used to adjust the input or output to the model;

(d) that productivity is related to 'average' skill rather than that of particular individuals;

(e) that output, in manpower effort, is converted to cost using forecast rates and adjusted for inflation where appropriate;

(f) that adequate time is allowed in the estimating schedule for running the model.

Step 10 — Check on skilled staff. The number of staff available with knowledge of the software tools, methodology and application must be checked. The level of skill and availability for the project should be checked. Any shortfall will have to be made up by:

(a) training in the relevant systems;

(b) arranging for skilled contract staff to be used on the project.

Both of these will involve a cost that must be estimated and included.

Step 11 — Identify unknowns. Any aspects of the project for which there is no skill base, no established technical solution or historic data should be identified so that unknown and doubtful areas can be addressed in an objective way.

Step 12 — Forward inflation rates. Projects which extend over more than one fiscal year will need to include an allowance for inflation and appropriate rates should be agreed for the period of the project.

Step 13 — Exchange rates. If the project involves the purchase of resources from another country or project staff travelling to another country then exchange rates for those items must be agreed and used in the costing.

Step 14 — Linking design, estimating and planning. The elements of the TIC will be directly related to the nature of the proposed systems and be influenced by the structure of the design. It is also essential at this stage to link estimating with the planning process so that the costs of activity-based elements can be distributed on a corresponding time basis to the project plan. The close link between estimating, design and planning must be maintained at all times with an interchange of information between them as indicated in Figure 5.1.

Step 15 — External purchases. In addition to the activity elements there may be elements, such as the purchase of software licences, that will incur a cost but no manpower — these must be set out over the timescale of the project as secondary elements for each main element of the TIC with appropriate allowances included for inflation and/or exchange rates. Equipment or other resources for which there is a monthly, or quarterly, charge should be included and the costs distributed over the timescale in which they will be incurred. Capital purchases of equipment or other project resources should be included in the schedule. It is important that these are scheduled to correspond with corporate policy — in some instances this may be at the time of purchase, i.e. commitment, and not the later time of delivery or payment.

Step 16 — Built-up cost estimate. The information prepared in the foregoing steps can now be brought together to prepare the elements of the TIC as illustrated in Appendix III. Each element should be distributed over the appropriate part of the project timescale to give a built-up cost profile. Tables 6.2 to 6.10 illustrate the project cost elements and the cost profile using the TIC template spreadsheets given in Chapter 4. The example used is that given in Table 4.15 for replacing an existing maintenance management system by a customised version of an off-the-shelf package. The benefit from use of the system is set out in Table 6.11.

Step 17 — Review and reiteration. The built-up cost arrived at over steps 1–16 must be reviewed with the system design and with the project plan. Changes in any one area will affect the others and it is important in carrying out any further iteration that all three aspects are kept fully in step.

The single objective is to produce the best estimate of the cost of

Table 6.2 Total installed cost template — assessment

Primary cost elements	Elapsed time from start — in quarter years										Total
	1	2	3	4	5	6	7	8	9	10	
Justification:											
study team	30,000	30,000									60,000
consultants	10,000	10,000									20,000
Technical feasibility:											
study team		20,000	50,000								70,000
consultants		20,000	20,000								40,000
prototyping											
Macro estimating			5,000								5,000
Cost−benefit assessment			5,000								5,000
Assessment costs	40,000	80,000	80,000								£200,000

Table 6.3 Total installed cost template — requirements definition

Primary cost elements	Elapsed time from start — in quarter years										Total
	1	2	3	4	5	6	7	8	9	10	
Preparation of functional specification			35,000	20,000							55,000
Review of functional specification				5,000							5,000
Infrastructure specification				10,000							10,000
Preparation of statement of requirements			10,000	15,000							25,000
Evaluation of statement of requirements				40,000							40,000
Preparation of invitation to tender				5,000							5,000
Evaluation of responses to invitation to tender				10,000							10,000
Requirements definition			45,000	105,000							£150,000

the proposed software in the context of the design, construction and implementation based on the input available.

The estimate needs to be set out and used in a consistent, itemised way for the following reasons:

(a) information for the built-up estimate may come from more than one source and errors can be introduced if such inputs are arbitrary, 'adjusted' or reapportioned over TIC elements or over the timescale;

(b) the built-up estimate will almost certainly require approval and

Table 6.4 Total installed cost template — design

Primary cost elements	Elapsed time from start — in quarter years										Total
	1	2	3	4	5	6	7	8	9	10	
System specification					8,000						8,000
System prototyping											
Detailed requirements specification					8,000						8,000
Architectural design											
Module design and specification					10,000						10,000
Software design and specification					10,000						10,000
Specification of system tests					2,000						2,000
Design and specification of acceptance tests											
Specification of documentation					2,000						2,000
Specification of data transfer/take-on											
Design costs					40,000						£40,000

Table 6.5 Total installed cost template — development

Primary cost elements	Elapsed time from start — in quarter years										Total
	1	2	3	4	5	6	7	8	9	10	
Software coding and unit testing					30,000						30,000
Module testing					18,000						18,000
Subsystem linking and testing					5,000						5,000
System integration					2,000						2,000
System interface testing					5,000						5,000
On-line help testing					5,000						5,000
User documentation					10,000						10,000
System documentation					5,000						5,000
Development costs					80,000						£80,000

budgetary sanction from general management — this may give rise to queries regarding some elements or changes may be required in the cost distribution to suit overall fiscal constraints;

(c) estimates may need to be revised at a later date due to changes in specification — this often happens just before the project starts or soon after it is under way;

(d) the effort and cost estimates need to be compared with the actual effort and cost as essential material for the review process — this will provide the input to the database for *future* estimating and the objective must be to strive for constant improvement.

Table 6.6 Total installed cost template — implementation

Primary cost elements	Elapsed time from start — in quarter years										
	1	2	3	4	5	6	7	8	9	10	Total
Preparation and loading of acceptance test database					20,000						20,000
Functional acceptance testing					5,000						5,000
Stress testing					5,000						5,000
Installation and commissioning					5,000						5,000
Data clean-up and restructuring					10,000	20,000	20,000	20,000	15,000		85,000
Database loading						10,000	5,000	5,000	5,000		25,000
Manual data loading						10,000	5,000	5,000	5,000		25,000
Operational acceptance testing						5,000					5,000
Fault listing and fault rectification						5,000	5,000				10,000
Decommissioning of existing system							5,000		5,000	5,000	15,000
Implementation costs					45,000	50,000	40,000	30,000	30,000	5,000	£200,000

Table 6.7 Total installed cost template — training

Primary cost elements	Elapsed time from start — in quarter years										
	1	2	3	4	5	6	7	8	9	10	Total
Training of project team											
Design and loading of training database				5,000							5,000
Preparation of training programme					20,000						20,000
Training of operational support staff					10,000						10,000
Training of help desk					5,000						5,000
Training of users						20,000	25,000	40,000	35,000	20,000	140,000
Training costs				5,000	35,000	20,000	25,000	40,000	35,000	20,000	£180,000

Table 6.8   Total installed cost template — project management and administration

Primary cost elements	Elapsed time from start — in quarter years										Total
	1	2	3	4	5	6	7	8	9	10	
Project management	3,000	3,000	3,000	10,000	10,000	10,000	10,000	10,000	10,000	7,000	76,000
Project administration		500	500	1,000	2,000	2,000	2,000	2,000	2,000	2,000	14,000
Administrative hardware				500				500			1,000
Administrative stationery				200	200	200	200	200			1,000
Accommodation at project site											
Accommodation at remote site											
Travel and subsistence costs											
QA, QC and audit											
Cost estimating and project accounting	1,000	500	500	500	500	200	200	200	200	200	4,000
Project planning and project control	500		700	1,000	500	500	200	200	200	200	4,000
Staff recruiting costs											
Project management and administration costs	4,500	4,000	4,700	13,200	13,200	12,900	12,600	13,100	12,400	9,400	£100,000

Table 6.9   Total installed cost template — operational software

Primary cost elements	Elapsed time from start — in quarter years										Total
	1	2	3	4	5	6	7	8	9	10	
CAD package											
DBMS					20,000		20,000	20,000		10,000	70,000
Graphics package											
System security software											
Operational environment											
Applications package					80,000		50,000	25,000		25,000	180,000
Operational software costs					100,000		70,000	45,000		35,000	£250,000

Table 6.10 Total installed cost template — cost profile

Primary cost elements	Elapsed time from start — in quarter years										Total
	1	2	3	4	5	6	7	8	9	10	
Assessment	40,000	80,000	80,000								200,000
Requirements definition			45,000	105,000							150,000
Software tools											0
H/W facilities for development											0
Design					40,000						40,000
Development					80,000						80,000
Implementation					45,000	50,000	35,000	35,000	30,000	5,000	200,000
Training				5,000	35,000	20,000	25,000	40,000	35,000	20,000	180,000
Project management and administration	4,500	4,000	4,700	13,200	13,200	12,900	12,600	13,100	12,400	9,400	100,000
Operational software					100,000		70,000	45,000		35,000	250,000
TIC	44,500	84,000	129,700	123,200	313,200	82,900	142,600	133,100	77,400	69,400	£1,200,000

Table 6.11 Benefit assessment

Item	Benefit per year
Reduction in manpower	1,500,000
Reduction in inventory	850,000
Reduction in direct materials	300,000
Saving in transport	250,000
Saving in IT costs	100,000
Total benefit	£3,000,000

6.10 Adjusting the output

The best estimate for a project is a realistic estimate which is based on the best input data available, assembled in an objective way without personal influence or adjustment. However, the 'best' estimate may not be the one which emerges from the estimating process and what eventually becomes the project budget may have been arrived at by adjusting the output from a model or other estimating process.

The pressures to adjust cost estimates on an arbitrary basis are often very significant and unrealistic. McNichols (23) quotes the following as typical questions posed immediately an estimate has been prepared:

• Can we do the work in half the time?
• Can we do the work for half the money?

- Can we do more work for the same money?
- What risk is there in your estimate?

Whatever the answer is to these questions it usually follows that some adjustment is made to the output for no objective reason.

Cover (5) considers that a manager's desire to please often prohibits objective cost estimates being put forward. Staff are forced to comply with overly optimistic estimates which in turn lead on to a low-quality or an incomplete product. Schedule is another candidate for manipulation but compressing the timescale causes imbalances in project staffing with consequent wasted effort. Another effect of the compression of timescales is that work that should be done in series has to be undertaken in parallel with a high probability that some of the work will have to be redone or possibly discarded altogether. Arbitrary changes of this kind are always counter productive and always lead to an increase in costs, which is quite the opposite of what the instigators imagined. Cover stresses that it is important that managers respect the estimating process and recognise it as the beginning of the process of project control.

Boehm (11) puts forward price-to-win as an estimating technique that is used by many organisations, in the past and the present and probably the future. The example quoted is an estimate for a job at $2 million where the customer has only $1 million in the budget. The estimator's task is to fix up an adjusted cost estimate that looks credible. This type of situation is becoming less tenable today when a larger part of the TIC is made up of direct costs for purchase of third-party software for development and operational support. The price-to-win approach is not confined to commercial situations — it is often the basis on which an IT department will put forward a cost estimate to a user department. They have the advantage of being able to omit elements of the total installed cost which can be regarded as general overheads, e.g. cost of CASE tools, DBMS, etc. These cannot be excluded by a contractor and this often results in a wide variation in the estimates for a project when internal and external estimates are compared. However, even for in-house estimates this approach is becoming increasingly difficult because now the cost of software tools has to be apportioned directly to the user applications.

Boehm (11) stated that

> the main reason that the price-to-win technique continues to be used is because the technology of software cost estimating has not provided powerful enough techniques to enable software customers or software developers to convincingly differentiate between a legitimate estimate and a price-to-win estimate.

However, by adopting the TIC approach a more powerful basis can be established that will make it much clearer to all concerned what has or has not been included and where the differences in estimates are arising.

Any adjustment to output, from the best estimate TIC discussed in the foregoing, must be seen in context. The 'adjusted' estimate is not going to provide a satisfactory basis for a project budget or for project cost control purposes.

Furthermore it has no validity for a post-project review, because comparing the budget, based on an adjusted cost, with actual costs has no meaning. Finally it must be said that under no circumstances should any adjusted cost data be entered into an estimating database.

6.11   Cost profile

So far what has been discussed in terms of the TIC is a cost profile. For internal projects where no 'invoice' as such is involved this may be all that is required. However, senior management should take a keen interest in this profile from three standpoints:

1. What part of the cost will be external (i.e. paid to third parties) and when will this payment be incurred in the overall timescale?
2. At what stages in the project will there be something tangible and deliverable to justify the costs incurred?
3. When will the system be commissioned and the benefits which justify the investment begin to accrue?

Senior management will also want to examine the cost profile in the context of other commitments and may seek a change in the profile to spread the costs in a different way. Where a large commitment is involved, management may demand a development plan that produces tangible deliverables, at an intermediate stage, to set against the costs. This is a 'comfort' factor and gives some reassurance that part of the value of the system can be achieved as early in the overall schedule as possible and thus provide a return on the investment. The changes may take the form of a scaled-down initial specification or Mark 1 version of the proposed system with other facilities being developed as later, follow-through, phases.

Whatever form any such changes take another iteration of the project plan and cost estimate will be required. This will be made easier if the procedure set out in the foregoing has been used so that adjustments can be made at any level, or to any module, and be correctly reflected in the revised built-up cost. In practice, Tables 6.2 to 6.10 can be set up on a spreadsheet so that the revision of costs and changes to the timescale can be done very quickly. An important point to

Table 6.12 Cash flow profile — all figures times £1,000

Elapsed time (in years)	1		2		3		4		5	
Elasped time (in half years)	1	2	1	2	1	2	1	2	1	2
Total installed cost	−129	−253	−396	−276	−146					
Software licences				−12		−15		−30		−30
Support costs				−5	−5	−5	5	−5	−5	−5
Cost profile	−129	−382	−778	−1,071	−1,222	−1,242	−1,247	−1,282	−1,287	−1,322
Benefit profile					250	250	500	1,000	1,500	1,500
Cash flow	−129	−382	−778	−1,071	−972	−742	−247	718	2,213	3,678

make at this juncture is that the process of revising costs is an objective attempt to arrive at a satisfactory basis for funding the project and is a very different process from that discussed under the heading 'output adjustment' which is an arbitrary alteration to the estimate. Restructuring of the design or the project plan will in many instances lead to an increase in the overall estimate of project costs but may well result in an improvement in the cash flow for the project and fit better into the overall corporate fiscal plan.

For projects that are for a customer who is paying, the cost profile has to be examined against the payment schedule to establish the cash flow profile.

6.12   Cash flow

Cash flow is important from two standpoints

- assessment of the project as an investment
- viability of the project during the development.

The project as an investment was discussed at some length in Chapters 1 and 2. If a proper justification was carried out at the start of the project then the basic information will have been prepared at the Assessment stage. The benefits should now be reviewed and firm figures agreed. Any once-off benefits should be quantified and the relevant point, in the project timescale, at which the benefit will be gained should be identified. In general the benefits are assessed on an annual basis and presented as in Table 6.11, which in this example have been estimated at £3 million. The timescale over which the benefits will be gained should be identified and set out as a benefit profile over the appropriate part of the project timescale. In practice only a proportion of the total annual benefit from operational use of the system is likely to be gained in the initial years and that has been reflected in the benefit profile line of Table 6.12. In this example it has been estimated that about £500,000 can be gained in year 3 of the project, £1,500,000 in year 4 and the full £3,000,000 in year 5 from project start.

The investment cash flow profile, illustrated in Table 6.12, is based on the cost profile information from Table 6.10 and the benefit assessment discussed above. Assessment of the project as an investment can now be made from the information in Tables 6.10, 6.11 and 6.12. The key items of interest to management are as follows:

- total cost
- maximum negative cash flow
- payback period
- net benefit after a given period
- annual on-going return.

For the example used in this chapter the summary of these items is given in Table 6.13.

It is very important to keep the investment cash flow profile, as illustrated in Table 6.12, up to date throughout the progress of the project. Any changes in

Table 6.13 Summary of costs and benefits

Item	Benefit per year
Total cost	£1,200,000
Maximum negative cash flow	£1,071,000
Payback from commitment	3.5 years
Net benefit after 4 years	£718,000
Annual ongoing return	£3,000,000

the total cost and the cost profile will have an influence on the investment viability of the project and Table 6.13 should therefore be updated as a matter of course when any of the component figures change.

The viability of the project in terms of cash flow during the development, and prior to any benefit, is also important as there will be a period during which both contractor and customer will incur costs ahead of any return. Payment will normally lag behind the costs incurred and may be as follows:

- Proportions of the total cost at predetermined stages. This usually applies to fixed-price contracts.
- In monthly amounts directly proportional to the costs already incurred. However, the actual payment will always lag, by at least 2 months, behind the point on the schedule when the cost was incurred and will result in a negative cash flow for the contractor for most of the project.

A typical percentage distribution of costs for a project of 8 months' duration is given in Table 6.14. On the assumption that invoices are submitted in the month following the cost incurred and that payment is received 1 month later the cash flow is as shown: it is negative, peaks at 40% of total project cost and the full cost is not recovered until 2 months after the end of the project.

There is often a contractual clause allowing a 10% retention by the customer until the end of the warranty period of, say, 3 months has elapsed. This changes the cash flow for the contractor as shown in the lower part of Table 6.14: it peaks at 43.5% and the full cost is not recovered until 4 months after completion of the work.

Any delays in submission of invoices, any queries or delays in payment only exacerbate the situation as far as the contractor is concerned.

Some fixed-price contracts often have stage payments which reflect important milestones in the progress of the work. The first payment may be on signing the contract — this is usually to cover the purchase of hardware or software, from a third party, which is essential to the software development. This only has a marginal effect on the cash flow, which is not surprising since the customer is only going to pay against progress on the specific software commissioned.

The same project cost distribution is shown in Table 6.15 but with fixed-stage payments of which the first is a payment of 20% of total cost on signing the contract. It is assumed, in the example, that work starts immediately and the initial stage payment is not received until month 2. The cash flow in this case is much

Table 6.14 Cash flow profile as seen by contractor for payment against invoices

Elapsed time in months	Development period							Warranty period				
	1	2	3	4	5	6	7	8	9	10	11	12
Monthly costs (% of total)	5	10	20	20	20	15	5	5				
Invoice value		5	10	20	20	20	15	5	5			
Payment received			5	10	20	20	20	15	5	5		
Cash flow	−5	−15	−30	−40	−40	−35	−20	−10	−5	0		
Payment received			4.5	9	18	18	18	13.5	4.5	4.5	0	10
Cash flow (with 10% retention)	−5	−15	−30.5	−41.5	−43.5	−40.5	−27.5	−19.0	−14.5	−10	−10	0

less advantageous to the contractor with a peak negative cash flow of 60% of total cost. This example also includes a 10% final payment after 3 months' warranty so that the full recovery of costs is not until 4 months following completion of the project.

Every project has its own cash flow profile and it is important to establish that profile at the estimating stage so that the financial implications of the project can be examined and assessed. In reality the 'Hurray we have just won a £1 million contract' may well be seen by the contractor's financial controller as 'How can we possibly cope with a £600,000 liability'? The customer may also be concerned at the prospect of spending, say, £750,000 before anything is deliverable.

The main objective of the contractor is to cover costs and make a profit — to achieve this, costs should be recovered as quickly as possible.

The main objective of the customer is to have a working system for an agreed cost that will bring a return in a known period at an estimated level of risk — to achieve this, as much of the payment as is reasonable should be deferred until there are tangible deliverables.

Table 6.15 Cash flow profile for fixed-price contract with stage payments

Elapsed time in months	Development period							Warranty period				
	1	2	3	4	5	6	7	8	9	10	11	12
Monthly costs (% of total)	5	10	20	20	20	15	5	5				
Invoice value (for stage payment)	20		10			30		30			10	
Payment received		20		10			30		30			10
Cash flow	−5	5	−15	−25	−45	−60	−35	−40	−10	−10	−10	0

The customer does, however, have a vested interest in ensuring that the contractor does not become insolvent in the process of undertaking the development, particularly if that situation is caused directly by the cash flow of the project. It is not altogether surprising, therefore, that customers often require evidence of the financial position of a contractor to assure themselves that the contractor can cope with the project. It is surprising, however, that customers do not, as a matter of course, ask for a cash flow profile as part of the cost estimate.

In view of the outstanding debt position of most projects it also behoves contractors to assure themselves that the customer will remain solvent until all invoices have been paid. It is an interesting fact of life that in the construction industry more small firms become insolvent due to the customer's inability to pay for work, than due to their own estimating inadequacies or poor financial management.

In summary it can be said that the detailed estimate of the software costs and the corresponding cost profile and cash flow profile are intimately linked and, as mentioned previously, there is often a need to make changes after the initial estimating is completed. It is therefore crucial to the whole process that the cost profile and cash flow profile are set out in an orderly way that can be mapped directly with the TIC template so that the vital links between the design, the project plan and the commercial considerations can be kept in step from the early stages through to completion of the work.

6.13   Purchase of software packages

In Chapter 3 mention was made of commercially available software packages as an alternative to a custom system. The elements of cost for the purchase of software packages are identical to those described for a custom development; it is only the distribution of costs between the elements that is likely to be different. For example, a straightforward off-the-shelf installation will not involve any effort for design and development whereas a customised package will involve some effort and cost in these areas. In an estimate for the purchase of a package a significant proportion of the cost will arise in the operational software element. In addition to the licence cost for the application software there is also likely to be a significant cost for licensing support software for use with the package. High amongst these will probably be a DBMS and the associated costs for that will be derived in the following way:

1. A proportion of an existing DBMS licence may have to be picked up by the new application — it may be that the package was chosen because it fitted in with current corporate policy on DBMS use.
2. An existing DBMS licence may have to be extended to cover a different machine or different location — this additional cost must be borne by the new application.
3. A new DBMS licence has to be purchased for the application — if this is replacing an existing DBMS or file handling facility then licence costs for

both new and existing software may have to be included for the changeover period.

The process of detailed estimating described in this chapter can be used for all requirements, bearing in mind that the cost distribution will vary significantly between the elements for a custom development compared with an estimate for a package solution as can be seen in Table 2.1. Furthermore the TIC template approach can be used for estimating the overall costs of package software and comparing costs of different packages. In this way a high degree of consistency can be achieved for costing all software requirements and making comparisons of optional solutions.

When the cost estimate for the package has been completed a cost profile should be prepared, setting out the timescale over which the costs will be incurred. There may be a need to revise the cost estimate and the cost profile and, as indicated earlier in this chapter, there is always a benefit from improving an estimate by review and iteration and this applies just as much to package software as custom developments.

7 Project management and control of costs

7.1 Project management and control

As made clear earlier, this book is not about project planning and control techniques, but without a serious commitment to effective techniques and active project management there is little hope of controlling costs.

The appointment of a project manager is seen by many as the start of a project. This is quite wrong; the project has been under way from the conceptual stage and should be under continuous management from the point where the justification is examined through to post-project review. The project manager should oversee and influence the feasibility, requirements definition and the estimating process so that when the design and development work begins there is a full understanding of what has gone before. It is important that the project manager is fully conversant with the basis on which the project budget and project plan have been developed and the commitment made. At the point of making a commitment the project manager assumes control of all aspects of the work and this is reflected diagrammatically in Figure 7.1. Although the emphasis is now on the management of resources and control of the budget there will also be an ongoing requirement for estimating, planning and design resources.

Many people see 'project control' as a system for recording the expenditure of manpower, resources and cost on a progressive basis. Recording it for what purpose though? To pass to higher management — accord blame to those who prepared the estimates — or for its correct purpose which is to aid the management of the project to a satisfactory conclusion?

One factor in assessing the effectiveness of project management is to define clearly the measures of success. These are usually regarded as, simultaneously, the following:

- Meeting the requirement (specification).
- Delivering on time.
- Completing within budget.

As will be seen later, these are not absolutes related to the position at the time of approving the project plan and budget because there may well be external factors that influence the progress of the project in terms of time and cost. However, it is essential to set up a project on the basis that the estimated effort, productivity,

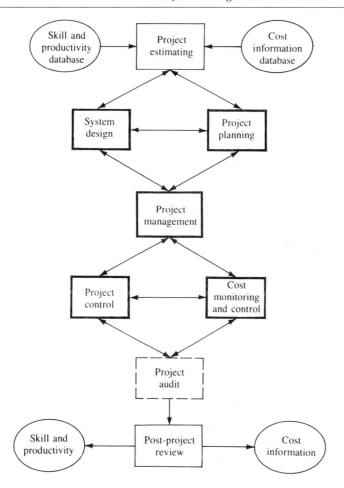

Figure 7.1
Project manager's
view of project

elapsed schedule and budget are realistic. All too often these are adjusted in some way in an attempt to ensure that the project budget looks 'acceptable'. However, this only places the project manager in a completely untenable position because no amount of attention to managing and exercising control will recover the situation and the project is doomed to exceed budget or timescale even before it begins. Keen (24) considers that much of this emanates from the inexperience of software engineers combined with a fear of higher-management attitudes if they are told that the target date or guideline budget they have set is unrealistic. Autocratic attitudes such as 'setting tough targets' and 'keeping people on their toes' are all much overrated and outdated management tactics which are not a substitute for realistic estimating and effective project control procedures.

Another important ingredient in the management and control of projects is to have clearly defined measures of progress. There are various approaches that are used, some more effective than others, the main ones being summarised below.

Control by expenditure of resources

This is where the use of resources is monitored against time and the consumption rate regarded as a measure of progress. In reality a lot of manpower effort can be expended for no effective progress and what is actually being recorded is the attendance of the project team, not the progress of the activities.

Control by budget

This is where costs are monitored against time and compared with the budgeted rate of spend. Assessing how much has been spent or is left is not a satisfactory way of measuring progress. Keen (24) likens it to 'measuring the amount of petrol left in the tank without considering how far is still to be travelled'.

Control by quality assessment

QC and QA are useful methods of control particularly in a production environment, but they must be based on some measurement which is either use of resources or costs or some combination. QA is in effect an independent assessment, from that of the project manager, but using the same sources of information and the same basis of measurement. It has the disadvantage that it is only periodic and is likely to indicate something useful when things have gone badly wrong rather than provide continuous monitoring and correction.

Control by accomplishment

Progress measured by the completion of previously defined steps provides a tangible and meaningful basis of assessment. If the distribution of the budget is related to those previously defined steps — milestones in the project — then actual costs can be compared with budget for a defined accomplishment. The dissenters from this approach consider it to measure progress in jerks as the reporting is only based on work actually completed at the reporting point. That is indeed true if the milestones represent substantial pieces of work but is easily overcome by breaking the work down into activities or groups of activities that can be completed within a timescale of no more than a month. The other disadvantage of this approach is that it understates the actual progress by not reporting on activities not completed at the time of making the assessment. But who can judge progress on uncompleted tasks? Baber (25) contends, and quite rightly, that 'it is essentially impossible for a programmer to estimate the fraction of the program completed ... how is he to guess whether the program is 40% or 50% complete?' Boehm (11) refers to Parkinson's law — work expands to fill the time available for its completion — and the deadline effect — the amount of energy and effort devoted to an activity is strongly accelerated as one approaches the deadline for completing the activity.

It follows that reporting progress on partially completed work can be very misleading in terms of the ultimate accomplishment of that activity. Summed over, say, 20 or 30 partly completed activities each month, 'estimating' intermediate progress can give a distorted picture of actual progress against both time and budget in the context of accomplishing the task. Estimated completion of activities can therefore give a false impression of progress on the project, month on month, and ultimately an impression that true progress is not known. The conclusion then conveyed is that the project is not being effectively managed which may be quite the reverse of the actual position.

7.2   Monitoring and reporting

Monitoring and assessing progress are continuing activities, not something to be done immediately prior to a monthly report. It must always be borne in mind that costs do not suddenly escalate one morning, nor does progress fall behind schedule without some cause such as a fall in productivity or shortfall in resources. This should be evident to everyone involved in management, both general management and project managers, and should not therefore come as a surprise in the monthly report. After all, the monthly report is only an echo of what should already be known and is not much good for monitoring or control if it is only prepared and circulated late in the following month and then only looked at by the recipient at an even later date!

Progress should be assessed weekly and reporting against budget and schedule done promptly on a monthly basis. Very large projects may be broken up into sub-projects that are run as semi-autonomous projects. These should report weekly within the project management structure and be aggregated as a whole project on a monthly basis. Such guidelines have served well in practice over a wide range of project types and sizes. However, each project should be judged according to the complexity of the technical innovation or the criticality of passing certain milestones and, where judged appropriate, more frequent assessment should be made at certain stages in the progress of the work.

Good project management is about the effective control of progress and the satisfactory completion of the work at the agreed cost.

Far too many software development projects are notable only for their runaway budgets and protracted timescales.

7.3   Staffing and productivity

The human resources dimension of project management is an important consideration in software engineering projects and can have a significant effect on completion of a project to the plan and cost estimate. One aspect is the recurring problem of skill shortage. Every advance in the development of software engineering tools, techniques and programming languages is followed by an immediate shortage of skills to apply these facilities. Staffing project teams may be adversely affected by three particular problems:

1. The availability of sufficient staff of the appropriate skill at the time required in the build-up of the team.

2. The retention of those skilled staff over the period required.
3. The replacement of skilled staff on a project in progress.

The initial project schedule and cost estimate will have been based on certain assumptions about the build-up of the team and productivity of team members in carrying out the various tasks. However, those assumptions may not be valid when the project is under way but some form of risk assessment should have been carried out that identifies the likely effects of the shortfall of skills and the impact of staff turnover.

Staff turnover

Every project should expect some level of staff turnover and if the project is of 6 months duration or longer it is highly probable. Various factors will influence the degree of turnover but personal satisfaction is a major ingredient that can be undermined by the following:

*   Undervalued skill coupled with strong market demand and more lucrative terms elsewhere.
*   Poor project management and poor perceived use of the personal skills.
*   Resources not available to individuals to do the job in an effective way.
*   Unsatisfactory location and conditions of work for the project team.

Everyone who leaves the team causes an overall drop in productivity, a disruption of the schedule, and a potential overrun. Staff who signal that they are intending to leave a project are of decreasing value and productivity and should be taken out quickly to minimise the overhead cost.

Acquisition of replacement

Getting staff of equivalent skill takes time — no one has skilled staff sitting around waiting to fill project slots. If the skill is scarce they will be off to find active work elsewhere and if not so scarce there will be a premium rate to pay for immediate availability.

Part of the project manager's brief should be to identify potential sources of skilled software engineers that can be drawn upon to mobilise replacements in the shortest possible timescale. Two things are important: replacement staff may not have the same level of skill as their predecessor — lower productivity — and they may have to drawn from a different source to previous staff and have a different (higher) unit cost.

Assimilation into the team

New members of a team, whatever their personal skill and experience, will need a period of time to become familiar with the project before becoming fully productive. In addition, a productive member of the team will have to spend some time with a new member and so there will be a further net drop in productivity before the benefit of the replacement staff is realised. A direct consequence is that the costs for the non-productive period of perhaps two team members (new and mentor) must be assessed and borne by the project budget.

It will be clear from the foregoing that the initial staffing and changing of staff can have a profound influence on the project schedule and budget. Much of this cannot be forecast and hence cannot be allowed for in the project plan and cost estimate. However, adding contingency is not a solution. At the estimating stage an assessment of risk should be made regarding staff turnover and skill shortage and an appropriate allowance should be included in the productivity of relevant parts of the manpower estimates. A simple, but effective formulation is:

$$\text{Expected productivity} = \text{Potential productivity} \times \text{Turnover effect}$$

Potential productivity is that which would be expected from skilled manpower contributing throughout the relevant period of the project.

Turnover effect is made up of the following:

Termination effect: period of reduced effectiveness.
Replacement delay: period with no skill available.
Assimilation effect: period of reduced effectiveness during assimilation. This should be doubled to allow for reduced effectiveness of a mentor.

The impact of reduced productivity will be greater on projects of short duration, but on longer projects there may be multiple occurrences of staff loss and the small effect in percentage terms will be potentially applicable across a wider range of the team.

Table 7.1 illustrates the overall effect on productivity of staff turnover. In practice this must be based on expected durations for each factor. In some instances it may take much longer to find replacement staff and for complex aspects of project development it may take longer for new members to be assimilated into the team and become productive.

The percentage loss of useful time should be applied as a percentage loss of productivity and be reflected as an increase in duration and cost for the relevant

Table 7.1 Loss of productive time compared with planned due to staff turnover

Planned staff duration (weeks)	Termination effect (weeks)	Replacement delay (weeks)	Assimilation effect (weeks × 2)	Total	Loss (%)
20	2	4	4	10	50
40	2	4	4	10	25
80	4	4	6	14	17
120	4	4	6	14	11

project activities. This process may need to be applied more than once in projects of long duration.

In order to recover potential overruns there is a temptation to increase staffing levels. This is on the assumption that people and time are interchangeable — this is a false premise which leads to all sorts of difficulties. There is an optimum manpower loading for any task or group of tasks. There are small margins around the optimum, but beyond these margins the effectiveness falls off and the cost will increase. The optimum manpower loading on a software module is dependent on access to facilities, the structure of the proposed software and the interaction between teams working on the whole development.

Brooks (an IBM Systems Manager) promulgated a law that states 'adding people to a late project only makes it later'. Indeed, adding more people at any stage is likely to affect adversely the timescale it is intended to improve. Adding more people is of course adding more cost.

7.4   Assessing progress

In many projects there is an uneven spread of effort and costs over the timescale of the work. The most important pointers to effective progress are assessments made at certain milestones — stages at which an activity or group of activities is completed or a review phase is reached. These milestones do not occur at uniform and convenient elapsed dates in the schedule but must be chosen at suitably close intervals to ensure that the assessment against project plan and budget is effective. It follows that the timescale is only of secondary interest in assessing progress. The key to success in monitoring progress is assessing resources used and expenditure against actual accomplishment of the work activities and then assessing the consequences of that situation in the context of the timescale.

The accomplishment cost procedure (ACP) put forward by Block (26) has been used very effectively for a wide range of types and sizes of software projects and has proved to be an effective method of presenting information for project control and project reporting.

Block's ACP, first published in 1971, was not specific to software projects and was not therefore geared to the software development procedures of that period. It continues to be relevant and effective as it covers manpower, and other resources used, on a unit basis, as well as single or multiple items of expenditure committed and payable to third parties. The ACP approach is fully compatible with the total installed cost format used as the basis for presenting estimates set out in Chapter 4. It is possible therefore to produce an actual cost profile and an actual cash flow profile from ACP for comparison with the estimated or budgetary figures produced using the TIC template.

7.5   Applying accomplishment cost procedures

The objective in ACP is to correlate costs with overall schedule accomplishment. Thus there is no specific reporting on 'progress' of tasks or activities not completed

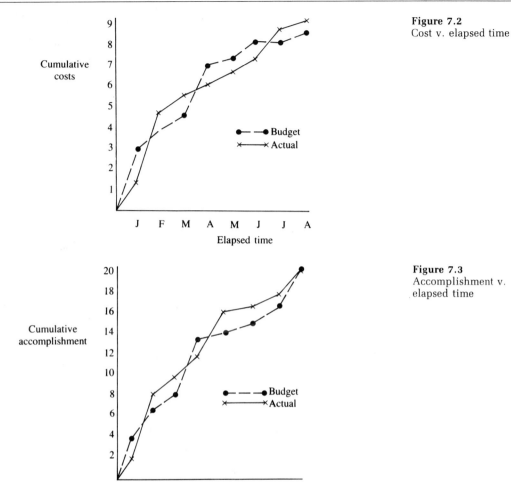

Figure 7.2
Cost v. elapsed time

Figure 7.3
Accomplishment v. elapsed time

— reference was made earlier to the problems of judging correctly progress on an activity that is incomplete. In the ACP progress on an activity is therefore reported at a milestone which does not necessarily have to coincide with a periodic review date, such as month end. The completed activities up to the review date are reported and activities that are still in progress are omitted.

Conventional cost reporting would look much as given in Figures 7.2 and 7.3 at review dates coinciding with, say, the end of the month. In accomplishment/cost reporting the report can be given nominally at the end of the month but relevant to some previous date coinciding with a milestone.

The accomplishment/cost report form is shown in Figure 7.4 for a resource use such as manpower or other resources used on a progressive basis against elapsed time.

Figure 7.4
Cost v.
accomplishment

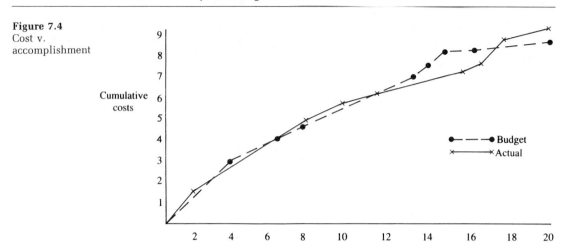

Table 7.2   Recording accomplishment and cost at milestones

	Budget (date)					Actual				
Milestone	Schedule date	Accomp. units	Cumulative accomp.	Cost units	Cumulative cost	Actual date	Accomp. units	Cumulative accomp.	Cost units	Cumulative cost
	Revised budget (date)					Actual carried forward				

Table 7.3   Summary of actual v. budget and action statement

Milestones	Budget cumul. accomp.	Actual cumul. accomp.	Budget cost	Actual cost	Schedule date	Cause of deviation	Action

The tabular format suited to this reporting procedure is given in Table 7.2 and an accompanying brief commentary, again on a milestone basis, should be prepared in a format such as that given in Table 7.3.

The important feature of this system of cost control is flexibility. Some change from the original estimate is inevitable and most likely to be associated with a revision to the staffing cost profile. This kind of change can be accommodated by revising the budget forward from an agreed milestone and indicating this by the insertion of a line in Table 7.2 as shown. No one is likely to be interested in actual accomplishment, against the previous budget from that date forward, but clearly the reasons for changing the budget must be recorded and this should be done on Table 7.3. This is a brief form of report particularly suited to the needs of senior management and provides a much better feel for project progress than having to wade through masses of numbers. Another aid to the immediate interpretation of ACP against budget and plan is given in Table 7.4. It is a useful *aide-mémoire* for those new to the ACP approach and is also useful to senior management who will not normally be looking at reports in this format on a day-to-day basis.

In addition to manpower and other resources used on a progressive basis throughout the project it is also necessary to record at appropriate milestones any third-party and capital costs, committed at those points and also when such lump payments are due. Aggregation of this information with the information in Table 7.2 will give a comprehensive actual cost profile of the project, on a progressive basis, for comparison with the estimated cost profile discussed in Chapter 6.

In conventional cost monitoring and control procedures people spend a lot of time looking at the numbers and very little thought or attention is given to their meaning in terms of the general health of the project. Interpretation of the numbers is often in the form of a long report 'explaining', or interpreting the masses of otherwise incomprehensible data. The real situation on the project may well be obscured by all this and one has to wonder whether that is often the intention! One important consequence of all this confusion is that the real cause of the problem on the project may be totally overlooked and decisions and action based on the information may be misdirected. More importantly, the reporting procedure

Table 7.4 Comparing accomplishment and cost with budget

Accomplishment	Cost	Date	Possible causes
Less	More	Early Late	Poor estimating Low productivity
Less	Less	Early Late	Overestimated Underresourced
More	Less	Early Late	High productivity Poor estimating
More	More	Early Late	Overresourced Underestimated

may obscure the wider cost implications of the situation. In ACP the situation overall can more readily be seen, causes of deviation from plan and budget identified, and action taken to set things back on course. However, it is important to recognise, particularly in projects of medium- or long-term duration, that every deviation from the plan is not necessarily a bad thing as it may be corrected in the short term without the need for action. Information provided by any project and budget control system is for guidance and the decision to take any action is ultimately up to the project manager.

7.6   Sources of change

The only certain thing in any business environment is that change will occur. It may come from within or be imposed from outside. Some changes are controllable, others cannot even be forecast. Examples of externally imposed change are economic boom and recession in particular sectors of the economy. Cuts in defence expenditure can lead to a significant slowdown in implementing project phases or in extreme cases cancellation of contracts. Boom time in the financial sector can create a situation where software is required for use on a much shorter timescale than originally planned to take advantage of a new, previously unforeseen, market opportunity. Change, due to economic circumstances, can also occur within the confines of the corporate environment and may have a direct effect on the funding of projects already sanctioned or projects currently in progress. Whatever the situation and no matter how the change arises there will be a need to re-examine and possibly revise the schedule, the cost profile and the cash flow profile for the project.

In some circumstances changes to the specification are identified as desirable and in the corporate interest, even after the project has started. There is the choice open to leave these changes aside to be incorporated as major follow-up enhancements or to change the specification of the current development. This will often be dictated by how far the project has progressed through the development cycle. If the changes are to be included in the current development project then it will be necessary to make changes in the project plan, project schedule and then appropriate revisions to the estimated costs.

7.7   Dealing with uncertainty

Those things which cannot be foreseen or are out of direct control may not seem worth discussing. Certainly specific action in any particular case must be a matter of judgement at the time. It is important to recognise that in many sectors of the economy IT and computer software in particular are bound inextricably into operational activities, and management decisions are dependent on information from such systems. There are some sectors and businesses that have fended this off but overall they are the losers in terms of company efficiency and effectiveness, and it is only a matter of time before economic necessity will force them to follow. IT in general and new software developments in particular can no longer be regarded as the first targets for cutback in times of recession and restructuring. Account needs to be taken of investment already made in the system development and the potential corporate loss of benefit if the system is not brought into operational use. Takeovers and mergers are likely to lead to the abandonment of some software developments in mid-stream at considerable cost and with an ongoing effect on morale.

Particular areas of uncertainty that can affect a software development include the following:

- Third-party software performance below expectations particularly where the project is dependent on the specific package.
- Third-party software not delivered to schedule.
- Hardware facilities not available for software development or commissioning; this includes local-area network (LAN) and wide-area network (WAN) telecommunication facilities.
- Industrial action by:
  - · project staff, which will affect the whole schedule;
  - · user groups, which may affect availability for consultation, conduct of acceptance tests and user training;
  - · airlines, etc., which may cause disruption to activities carried out at remote sites.
- 'Flu epidemics or other natural hazards.
- Corporate restructuring, takeovers and mergers.

Any action or event which disrupts the project schedule will most likely increase the project costs and delay the financial benefit from having the system in use. Profit margins are always small and any increase in costs will only erode those margins. Whilst no one can prevent such uncertain events occurring it is important that estimators, project planners and project managers become much more aware of the need to develop and use methods that will help them cope with the effects of such events, and to assess quickly the impact on the schedule and cost of the development.

7.8   Dealing with changes to the specification

Additions to the specification are typical of the changes imposed on projects in progress in the software industry. Some stem from the emergence of new technical facilities that seem either appropriate or exciting to have in the system. Most frequently specification changes come from situations where users have not thought through their needs or indeed may not have been consulted on a sufficiently wide basis to incorporate all of the detailed nuances of the application area.

Other changes to specification arise from corporate restructuring, or takeovers which necessitate embracing a wider application requirement in terms of both functionality and the number of locations from which the system will operate.

Whether specification changes are small or large they should be dealt with in a systematic way through a change control procedure which should involve the following steps:

- Identifying what is required functionally.
- Identifying the impact on the existing design and the current system status.
- Specifying how the changes will be made.
- Carrying out relevant design work.
- Estimating the effort and time involved, including any modification to planned tasks or repeating of tasks already completed.
- Estimating the costs involved.
- Revising the TIC and cost profile.
- Revising the cash flow profile.

Finally the system changes, revised cost and schedule will need to be sanctioned and an updated project budget agreed.

7.9   Innovation

Technical innovation, new techniques and methods are part of the everyday fabric of the IT industry — software as well as hardware. Innovation is not something that applies just to tools and techniques of software development but it also features in the facilities provided to meet the increasingly sophisticated demands of users. Where innovation is imposed as part of a change of specification then steps must be taken by the project manager to ensure that there is a clear understanding of what is involved technically, the risk involved in implementing the change and the effects on schedule and budget.

In any case innovative software engineering has a nasty habit of going wrong even if it has been tested, as well as subjected to rigorous design considerations. Although prototyping should be done before a project starts, it is nevertheless there as an aid if things do go wrong in the course of development. The lowest-cost solution is always to take an objective approach such as prototyping rather than just cast about randomly for a way to 'fix' a problem.

7.10   Accommodating change

Retrospective change in the timescale of a project is not just a matter of laying off or taking on more staff and altering the schedule dates.

To slcw a project down — due to recession or deferment of budget — requires a review of the project plan. It may be appropriate to reduce staffing levels or alternatively to introduce time breaks between phases. To speed up a project it may be appropriate to increase the number of staff or to overlap some phases of the work. There are, however, limits to making retrospective changes of this kind and attention must be given to the consequent change to the cost profile and the knock-on effect to the cash flow profile and ultimately the estimated benefit.

If budget and schedule changes are made and agreed for any reason, then that situation should be made clear to all concerned. All too often changes of this kind are not communicated effectively and ideas prevail that projects are seriously overrunning when that is not the correct situation.

7.11   Interpretation of accomplishment/cost information

The interpretation of information in terms of action or reaction depends on the viewpoint taken — customer or contractor — and in relation to the broader plan of commitments and priorities.

Being ahead of schedule and over budget, but on target, may cause the following problems:

* The customer accounts department may be unwilling to pay invoices at a value higher than budgeted even though the work has been done satisfactorily.
* The customer may not have target hardware in place or interfacing tests cannot be done ahead of schedule. The contractor cannot redeploy all of the staff to other work and consequently higher productivity or overresourcing, compared with the project plan, will incur additional costs to the contractor.

Late delivery is more likely to be accompanied by overspending. Overruns on project budgets are usually due to lower productivity than estimated and should not be confused with a situation that is underresourced. Late delivery will almost certainly incur additional costs for the contractor, eroding profit. However, the consequences may also be higher costs for the customer, particularly where there is interfacing with other developments and where other teams may be working to another schedule covering the commissioning of the whole system.

Late delivery can have wider and more significant cost implications. The customer commissioned the software to use in the operational business environment where its use will either save costs or assist in making additional income. Until the software is commissioned these objectives cannot be realised. Indeed, it is crucial that attainment of the benefits from the system is kept under review, and each time there is a revision to the project costs, there must be a corresponding revision of the cash flow profile and cost−benefit assessment. Far too many projects are set up with only marginal return on the investment. This is lost sight of once the project gets under way, and any budget increases or extension of the timescale can quickly erode that benefit and result in a project that has negative net benefit. Even for projects that are expected to yield a significant return on the investment constant vigilance is necessary to ensure that the net benefit is maximised.

8 Project audit and post-project review

8.1 Need for an audit

Much of what has been said earlier in this book has been aimed at raising the value of software by ensuring that it meets a business requirement in terms of an effective return on the investment. In earlier chapters we have looked at the estimating process, its link with project planning and the follow-through into project management and control. If these are done well and are all treated as linked and compatible activities then a good foundation will have been laid down for a successful project. However, there is also a need to look at how the project is progressing on a continuing basis.

Just as in the case of design review, which is an independent assessment of how the need will be met, there is also a need for formal project review to make an independent assessment of how the development of the system is progressing. Part of that must be concerned with review of the technical system itself, but equally important is the review of progress against the project plan and the spend against the budget.

Project audit is often seen as censure of what is going on with the sole objective of finding fault, but the software industry must look forward and regard the project audit process in the same way that we have formal financial audit of every organisation. The outcome of most corporate financial audits is simply a formal statement that all is in order and the software industry should start to work towards a similar situation in the audit of software engineering projects.

Those organisations who already have formal quality assurance (QA) procedures in place, and in use, will be familiar with project audit procedures and know that they do not interfere with the progress of the project and often come up with useful suggestions on matters that need attention. Such audits always provide a measure of reassurance to the project manager, and to general management, that all is progressing well on the project. Non-interference with the progress of the project does of course presuppose that records on accomplishment and costs are up to date for the work already completed and that there is satisfactory evidence that the remaining work of the project can be done within the budget and timescale.

Overall, quality management systems are the vehicle for putting methods into practice. The UK Department of Trade and Industry (DTI) see quality management systems as the route to ensuring that customers' expectations are met and reflect their business environment and culture. The DTI Guide to Software Quality

Management Systems (17) includes an appendix which sets out the Professional Attributes/Performance Standard for Software Quality Management Auditors. In the context of total quality management (TQM), quality management systems embrace the three main driving components:

1. Management commitment to improvement.
2. Motivation for improvement.
3. Measurement for improvement.

The project audit and review procedures are essential tools in the process of measurement for improvement but they must not be seen as procedural impositions from outside but as part of a new cultural ethos that is directed at achieving quality.

8.2   Purpose of an audit

If the procedures set out previously have been followed and periodic (monthly) reporting indicates that everything is on schedule and no problems are foreseen it is not unreasonable to ask why an audit is needed at all. The answer is simple — just as with corporate financial audit, an independent assessment provides confirmation of a satisfactory situation. However, the audit or review process has a number of specific uses which include the following:

- A routine audit, covering all QA requirements, should be part of the standard project procedures for software development.
- A recovery audit should be carried out when any significant deviation from plan or budget is identified or when any major change in specification is required.
- A post-project review should be carried out at the end of *all* projects and is the source of new information for the estimating database.

These three types of audit will have different objectives and the emphasis in the audit report will be different. However, the format and the way in which these audits are carried out should be consistent.

All audits should be carried out by staff who are independent of the project team. Where there is a QA department they will carry out most audits and if appropriate draw on other specialist skills as required. It is, however, essential that the project manager is fully involved and kept fully informed throughout the audit. The project team should also be fully appraised of the outcome — they need the feedback whether it is good, bad or indifferent news. The only grounds on which an audit should be carried out in secrecy is if there is some suspicion of fraudulent activity or possible infringement of corporate security. Always remember that an audit is essentially about measurement for improvement and confidential reports contribute nothing to that goal — openness is a major incentive to continued improvement in quality.

Once a project has been mobilised then revision to estimates, whether time or budget, becomes a project management responsibility as opposed to an estimating responsibility. That does not imply that there should be strict demarcation or barriers. The point is responsibility rather than process — the process should be that set out earlier for estimating, planning and project control.

Many organisations have change control procedures in place. These are often used for every type of change that occurs in the project but they are often stretched too far and are then not effective. A good way to break down change is as follows:

- Small technical changes, additions and amendments to the specification, etc., should be dealt with by change control procedures.
- Normal staff turnover, small changes in availability or access to resources should be dealt with as part of routine project management.

Both should be reflected as appropriate changes in the schedule and budget.

All other forms of change, whether arising from technical, staffing or other resource effects and irrespective of whether they are internal or imposed from outside, should be treated as a special audit. This is because they are likely to have a significant impact on the project and will require approval from senior management for a revised schedule and budget.

8.3   Routine audit

The purpose of a routine audit is to look at all work in progress and report on the technical aspects, work schedule, staffing, management and costs. A routine audit may be carried out at any time and those familiar with QA will know that this can be soon after start-up, or any time up to installation of the system. On long projects, or projects which are judged to have a high-risk element, there may be several routine audits carried out either at milestones or randomly.

The deliverables from a routine audit should be a brief commentary on technical matters, staffing, accomplishment, forward schedule and cost profile. Any areas of concern should be specifically highlighted with an indication of the effect on delivery of the planned system. If any serious shortcomings are identified in the course of a routine audit they should be recorded and the audit should be concluded by the preparation of a project recovery report.

8.4   Recovery audit

A recovery audit should be initiated when things have gone seriously wrong or some event has precipitated a serious interruption to the progress of the project. Recovery audits may be precipitated by any of the following:

1. Poor design, planning and estimating.
2. Use of innovative techniques without proper investigation or contingency planning.
3. Poor project management.
4. Shortcomings in third-party software or services.
5. Staff attrition higher than expected.
6. Political or natural hazard.
7. Corporate restructuring.

Items 1 and 2 are avoidable if proper attention is given to these matters in the early stages of the project and the justification, feasibility and estimating steps are carried out satisfactorily.

Shortcomings in project management may be manifest in a number of ways such as discontent in the project team resulting in low productivity and leading on to high attrition. Also, monthly reports may indicate that there are deviations from the schedule and budget for no apparent reason.

Third-party software may fall seriously behind schedule or fall short of expected performance. Third-party services, particularly technical staff, may not be satisfactory — in number, skill and hence productivity.

No one can foresee a competitor opening up near by and attracting away scarce skilled staff. Political or natural hazards cannot be forecast nor can the effect be ignored if they impinge directly or tangentially on the activities of a project.

Internal corporate restructuring and takeovers may necessitate a review of particular projects which may result in a radical change in the software facilities or even abandonment.

The key things to be addressed in a recovery audit, and to be included in the audit report, are as follows:

- Identification of the changes proposed or other causes for deviation from the agreed plan and budget.
- Identification of the effects in terms of the:
  - design;
  - technical effectiveness;
  - operational performance of system;
  - work plan and schedule;
  - overall cost and cost profile.
- Financial consequences of no action.
- Identification of any alternative courses of corrective action.
- Financial implications of making the changes in terms of risk, exposure and impact on the original justification.

8.5   Project review

The software industry is not renowned for learning from past experience — far too many software development projects end with commissioning of the system. Apart from those staff involved in ongoing support of the system, all the others rush forward to the next development, other jobs, or promotion. Whatever knowledge and experience was gained is largely neglected in terms of a formal project review. Valuable information on technical matters — how and how not to apply a particular technique or solve a particular problem again — are left in the memories of individuals but, as mentioned in Chapter 3, people are not good stores of information and much detail can be lost even over relatively short timescales. Information on schedules, productivity and costs is all too often not captured and reviewed, yet this is the most useful source of material for future estimating. The cycle of poor estimating, poor project control and cost escalation can be broken by instituting a process of post-project review. There must therefore be an obligation on every project team to carry out a post-project review and capture all relevant information in a form usable by others.

The post-project review is a terminal audit of the project with the objective of establishing actual effort, productivity, time and costs and comparing these against the planned manpower schedule, timescale and budget. The objectives of the post-project review in terms of software costing are as follows:

- To establish the final cost of the project.
- To establish the actual cost/benefit based on the final position and assess this against the original expectations.
- To identify any actions necessary to ensure that the attainable benefits are maximised.
- To identify any factors that have helped or impaired the progress of the project that should be taken into account and used to improve the cost control of future projects.
- To prepare data from the project for use in future estimating.

The functional role of the post-project review, and the project audit, is illustrated in the context of the whole project cycle in Figure 8.1.

There is often a reluctance to devote effort to a post-project review but committing a small amount of time, effort and financial resources at this point in the whole cycle is likely to be much more effective whilst memories are fresh and project records still intact.

The accomplishment cost procedure (ACP) records, discussed in Chapter 7 for cost control of the project, provide a good basis for carrying out the post-project review. In Chapter 7 mention was made of the compatibility between the TIC template and the ACP records and it was indicated that the TIC template should be mapped on to the ACP records. In the post-project review the reverse process can take place. This will provide a final cost profile in the TIC template format that can be combined with the benefits profile to give a final cash flow profile. The timescale for return on the investment can be examined and any actions set in train that will ensure the benefits are realised as quickly and as fully as possible.

A general report on the project should be prepared that addresses all aspects of the project covering the following:

- Design.
- Specification.
- Development.
- Implementation.
- Tools and facilities.
- Staffing.
- Third-party facilities.
- Project management.

The report should be objective and not be seen as a vehicle for apportioning blame

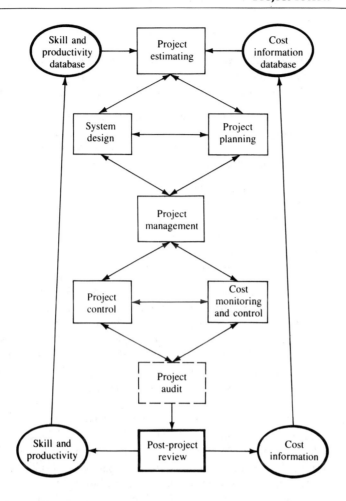

Figure 8.1
Post-project review

for deviations from plan and budget. It should comment on why changes were necessary, how they were implemented, the outcome of these actions and any lessons learned for the future. Improving the cost effectiveness of software engineering is not just about better models or better numbers — it is also about better practices.

DeMarco (3) recommends that much more attention be given to the recording of information at the end of a project and suggests the following scope for post-project records:

- Project charter.
- Specification model.
- Metric analysis of specification model.
- Design model.
- Metric analysis of design model.
- Version plan.

- Metric analysis of version plan.
- Delivered code.
- Metric analysis of delivered code (volume and complexity).
- Cost by activity, function, module and class of work.
- Metric analysis of maintenance characteristics of the delivered code.

This is much more comprehensive than is usually prepared at the end of a project. Indeed it could well form the basis of a good standard for post-project records so that the record set as a whole can be used for the following in addition to the requirements of the post-project review:

- Software cost estimating database.
- Software operational support.
- Configuration management and control.
- Software life cycle database (system archive).
- Software life cycle costing.
- Post-implementation benefit audit.

One of the aims in a post-project review is to reduce the risk in future estimating through the process of measurement for improvement. The first point to note from the estimating standpoint of a post-project review is that the only valid basis for comparison is a best and realistic estimate for the project. 'Adjusted' estimates, referred to in Section 6.10, *have no validity* for the post-project review and will only cause confusion because there will appear to be unrealistic variances between estimate and actual and no useful judgement can be made on the accuracy of the original estimating.

Another important consideration in carrying out a post-project review is that in comparing actual costs with estimates, the estimates must be the final version which may have been completed part of the way through the project. In some extreme cases the final estimate may have been prepared as a result of a recovery audit — in this event careful consideration will need to be given to the validity of data for future estimating. The 'final' estimate must reflect the 'final' specification and in many instances is unlikely to be that approved as the project start-up budget and may be made up from a mixture of the original estimate, up to a certain date, and then a revised estimate from one or more subsequent dates, including any changes covered in the change control procedure.

This may sound complex and involve a lot of retrospective analysis but little additional effort is needed if the accomplishment/cost procedure (ACP), discussed in Chapter 7, is used. The estimating information needed can therefore be lifted directly from the project control records that will have been prepared on an ongoing monthly basis and completed at the end of the project.

Having established that the estimates are a sensible record of the system specification 'as built', that is taking in changes as well as the original requirement, the next points to examine are the actual records of effort and expenditure and to establish from the project records if there have been any events that could distort the figures and make them invalid for future estimating purposes. These might include the following:

- Unusually high staff turnover not expected when the estimates were prepared.
- Industrial action.
- Significant delay in getting access to resources.

There is little point in recording manpower effort and productivity for future estimating if the data is not representative of 'normal' conditions of working. It may well be possible to compensate for the particular distorting effect, such as those mentioned above, or even leave out the activities most seriously affected.

A 'normalised' version of the TIC template can be prepared for future estimating purposes as the information can be used directly if an analog model is used. However, it must be clearly marked as such and annotated where changes have been made. Any changes to the actual figures, lifted from the end of project records, turns them into 'estimates' rather than actual figures and the value of the data is diminished greatly.

Timesheets, or other manpower records, together with the project plan will provide the basis for establishing the manpower effort used on different software development tasks and the associated productivity. The format in which this particular data is prepared will depend on the estimating database structure which itself is a function of the model in use — analog, algorithmic or function point.

8.6   Estimating — review loop

Throughout the preceding chapters the recurring emphasis has been on a consistent approach so that information generated at each stage can be mapped directly on to the next stage. Estimating feeds on to planning and then on to control. The final link is from project review back to estimating. Software costing is the poor relation in software engineering, but the key to more investment in software engineering tools and more effective operational systems will be dictated to some degree by our ability to manage the fiscal aspects of projects much more effectively.

Building better models and methods is a good aim but whatever the approach adopted there remains the need to focus a lot more attention on cost drivers and estimating parameters. The input to estimating databases can only come from past and current projects and consequently more time and resources have to be committed to the post-project review and it must become an essential part of project work that cannot be passed over as it has all too often in the past.

9 Influence of tendering on software cost estimating

9.1 Defining the objectives

Software cost estimating is of itself a difficult enough task but many problems of software costing are compounded in the tendering process. It is a well-established fact that the way in which pre-project activities are conducted, particularly those relating to the pre-contractual aspects, has a direct effect on the probability that the software will be produced satisfactorily and within the expected timescale and budget. Too few people take the trouble to identify why they are preparing an invitation to tender (ITT) and often fail to define, in the documents sent out, what objectives they have in seeking particular information in the responses. Four questions have to be addressed:

1. What is the software requirement and what options are acceptable?
2. Have the requirements been defined in a precise enough way for someone to estimate the work involved, the timescale for carrying it out and the cost?
3. On what basis is the assessment and comparison of responses to be made and how will a decision be reached that will ensure that the ultimate objective is reached — that of a robust, effective and efficient operational system?
4. What quality requirements are expected of the software? Are these explicitly defined so that a quality plan can be prepared?

In many instances invitations to tender are issued that demonstrate to a recipient that there is no clear idea of what is wanted — more a matter of guess what we want, at what price, from the few clues given in the ITT! — and at the same time the document is accompanied by commercial and contractual terms of a detailed nature. Poor definition manifests itself in two ways:

1. Vagueness about aspects of the system that will have a significant bearing on the design, timescale and cost of development.
2. Detailed definitions of parts of the system, or the way it should be constructed, that are often neither practical nor logical and are certainly not compatible with the vagueness in other parts of the document.

Where this occurs in an ITT it tells the recipient loudly and clearly 'I am not sure of what I want but you will do it the way specified'!

This approach to contracting out for software is of no value to either the customer or the contractor and what is quite clear, in this sort of situation, is that the customer is not yet in a position to issue an ITT and should be using some other formal basis for exchanging information that is not contractually binding on either party. It is to be hoped that this situation will rapidly disappear with much wider use, by both customer and contractor, of the principles set out in many of the new standards, guides and codes of practice now available to the software industry. The best option in the situation described above is to issue a statement of requirements (SOR), or operational requirement, and explore with potential contractors a satisfactory way forward for the proposed development and also who is best placed to work on it.

Whether it is an ITT or an SOR the single most important objective is to prepare a document that will motivate a good, well-thought-through technical and commercial response from the recipient. A good ITT or SOR, sent to a well-selected list of companies, will ensure that good responses are received and will pave the way to getting a satisfactory system developed, installed and operational.

9.2   The TQM approach

For those companies who have adopted and practise total quality management (TQM) the objective will be different from that discussed at the start of this chapter. The objective in preparing an ITT will be to install and commission a good-quality software system that meets a given specification, to an agreed schedule, at an agreed cost. The motivation from the outset is to achieve the end result and the various stages, including the tendering and system development, are only a means to that end, not an end in themselves.

9.3   Statement of requirements (or operational requirement)

Alternative ways of filling a particular software requirement are continuing to be more widely applicable so that there is less and less dependence on full custom development as a solution. Furthermore the need to prepare a detailed specification is less relevant with prototyping now becoming an effective alternative. Indeed there are many situations where a detailed specification is not necessary to achieve the objective, particularly where a package solution is the favoured option.

Issuing a statement of requirements, sometimes referred to as an operational requirement, is a formal, but non-contractual, way of opening up discussions with a potential contractor. The SOR is the only suitable format for the purchase of packages or core software. Many people, quite wrongly, issue an ITT embodying a specification detailing how they want a software package to perform the various functions. They are unlikely to find a satisfactory solution and what they should be defining in some detail is the functionality required by users.

There is no fixed format for an SOR but the following has been found, in practice, to be a good basis:

Introduction

A brief statement of the relevant business goals, the purpose of the proposed software in achieving those goals and any specific features of the requirement.

Objective

The particular requirement of the software system.

General features

A brief statement of the operational environment, user needs and support arrangements for the system.

Functional features

A brief statement of the application area highlighting the way in which data will be handled, enquiries made and reporting carried out. It is important to ensure that this is confined to 'need' not 'want', otherwise it will, like some specifications, become a 'wish list' and result in responses to the SOR that are for systems much larger than the real requirement and that indicate an unacceptably high level of cost.

Interaction with other systems

Very few software systems now function in isolation and an indication of the number and nature of the interfaces should be given.

Size and performance information

This should cover brief details of the file size and growth rate, transaction rate, the number of users and their geographic distribution, the response times for key functional features and database archiving requirements.

Human—computer interface

Stating that the system has got to be 'user friendly' is not much use to anyone. A brief description should be given of the operational environment — dusty, humid, industrial, or administrative — together with specific requirements for the following:

- Screen layout.
- Menus.
- Prompts.
- On-line help.
- User manuals.
- User training.

System features

Specific requirements regarding hardware, communications networks, operating systems, DBMS options and portability should be set out.

Support facilities

Information should be sought on how the system will be supported, licensing arrangements for any dependent third-party software etc.

Cost estimate

Although an SOR will not yield a binding quotation it is valuable to have a realistic estimate of the costs. This should be sought in the format of the TIC template for three reasons:

1. It will elicit cost estimates in a consistent format and ensure that nothing has been omitted. This is invaluable in ensuring that comparisons are fair and equitable between respondents.
2. It will indicate how the estimates for the different elements contribute to the estimated cost submitted by each respondent.
3. It will enable internal costs to be merged directly with the information provided in the responses to the SOR. The TIC template will then provide a consistent and full cost appraisal.

The summary of costs for a customised package from one potential contractor is shown in the TIC template format in Table 9.1. The summary form for a

Table 9.1 Tender for customised off-the-shelf package presented on TIC template

| Primary cost elements | Elapsed time from start — in quarter years | | | | | | | | | | Total |
	1	2	3	4	5	6	7	8	9	10	
Assessment											
Requirements definition software tools											
H/W facilities for development											
Design				40,000							40,000
Development				20,000	60,000						80,000
Implementation					10,000						10,000
Training					5,000	25,000	20,000				50,000
Project management and administration				7,000	10,000	2,000	1,000				20,000
Operational software				250,000							250,000
TIC				317,000	85,000	27,000	21,000				£450,000

Table 9.2 Comparison of four tenders for a customised version of an off-the-shelf package, together with TIC

Primary cost element	Tender A	Tender B	Tender C	Tender D	Estimate based on C
Assessment	—	—	—	—	200,000
Requirements definition	—	—	—	—	150,000
Software tools	—	—	—	—	—
H/W facilities for development	—	—	—	—	—
Design	60,000	20,000	40,000	10,000	40,000
Development	90,000	80,000	80,000	30,000	80,000
Implementation	15,000	20,000	10,000	15,000	200,000
Training	100,000	90,000	50,000	10,000	180,000
Project management and administration	25,000	30,000	20,000	10,000	100,000
Operational software	300,000	200,000	250,000	150,000	250,000
Comparative cost	£590,000	£440,000	£450,000	£225,000	—
TIC	—	—	—	—	£1,200,000

comparison of costs of four responses to an SOR for this package purchase is given in Table 9.2.

An alternative format and list of contents for an SOR is set out in appendix D of the UK DTI Guide to Software Quality Management Systems (17).

9.4   Specification or prototyping

Resulting directly from the SOR the customer may have three viable options:

1. Prepare an ITT, in simple format, where a product clearly matches the requirement to a significant degree and the cost estimate compares with a custom development. There may be a need to prepare a specification for:

    (a)   limited customisation or additions;
    (b)   interfaces to related systems.

2. Prepare a specification for tendering and select a shortlist of vendors from the responses to the SOR.
3. Commission a specification or prototype product. This will involve a much smaller-scale ITT than a full tender with consequent reduced overall risk and lower initial cost commitment.

Specifications appeal to contract managers and software engineers but have many shortcomings as far as the potential users of the system are concerned. A prototype product is a more dynamic representation and will give more confidence to users that their needs have been understood and that the proposed system will be effective. In terms of effectiveness Boehm *et al.* (21) carried out a comparative assessment of prototyping versus specification in 1983 and concluded the following:

- Prototyping yielded products with roughly equivalent performance but with 40% less code and 40% less effort.
- Prototyped products rated somewhat lower on functionality and robustness, but higher on ease of use.
- Specifying produced more coherent design and software that was easier to integrate.

Although prototyping has not been fully established as an alternative to specification there is little doubt that it will be used on a wider basis in the future. Indeed it is likely that systems will be defined by a combination of prototype and specification and subsequently developed with less effort and cost than at present.

At present there are far too many situations where contractors are expected to commit to contractual arrangements on the basis of poorly defined requirements. For the future it should be an aim of all concerned with the implementation of cost-effective systems to focus much more attention on the definition of requirements and investigation of the systems before launching into the tendering process.

Having a tight contractual commitment for a fixed-price job may sound impressive in that the contractor is required to bear any overrun on budget. However, an extended timescale to completion will result in a deferment in reaping the benefits of the system. Contracting for small stages of work that are each well defined has the advantage that a satisfactory system can be brought into operational use in the shortest possible timescale.

9.5   Tender lists

Irrespective of whether it is an ITT or an SOR there will normally be a list of companies to whom the document is sent as most situations are likely to be competitive tender. Unfortunately in too many cases the emphasis is on the *competition* and not the tender! Tendering and then developing a system to meet operational needs is a means to an end, *not* an end in itself. It is important therefore to look for potential contractors who can help achieve the objective of a satisfactory installed system, in the most cost-effective way. This does not mean the cheapest initial quote nor indeed the lowest tender, and anyone still hidebound by that approach is likely to be heading for serious trouble and inevitable escalating costs. It is much more useful to foster a degree of openness and build up mutual understanding and confidence in how the requirement can be met. Selecting the list of companies invited to tender should, therefore, be done with great care and the criteria should include the following:

- Relevant technical experience.
- Relevant project management experience.
- Satisfactory company financial performance.
- General suitability for the particular work.

In some instances this would seem to rule out small specialist companies and new emerging companies except for projects of a small size. This is not necessarily the case and full use should always be made of the best combination of skill and experience available. Generally speaking, purchasers of software systems do not make nearly enough use of consortia or contractor/subcontractor arrangements. The organisation preparing and issuing an ITT can have a major influence on bringing together a suitable grouping of skills which can have the advantage of the best technical solution on a good-value basis and meeting their own objective of quality software. Insufficient use is made of pre-qualification tendering, that is evaluating contractor skills outside the confines of a specific commercial tender. This is done by some organisations, such as UK government departments, on a periodic basis (annually, or biannually) or as a preliminary stage to a major contract. The aim is to become conversant with the technical skills, project management skills and financial standing of potential contractors and, where appropriate, formulate a list of preferred suppliers. Mutual understanding of business objectives and attitudes will ensure you have the best chance of motivating a good response to an ITT.

9.6   Realistic timescales

On all too many occasions ITTs are sent out before the pre-project tasks have been completed and, furthermore, ask for a response in a totally unrealistic timescale. Some organisations delude themselves that this 'keeps contractors on their toes', but what it is more likely to achieve is the following:

- That some potentially good contractors will drop out immediately.
- All potential contractors are likely to press immediately for an extension of the timescale.
- That delays will be involved before project start-up while the pre-project tasks are carried out retrospectively.

Unrealistic timescales do not give sufficient time for technical or commercial consideration of the project internally. This will be reflected in the low quality of the ITT, and it jeopardises the chance of getting a good-quality response.

The key stages in the pre-project timescale are as follows:

- Assessment of justification.
- Feasibility and macro cost estimate.
- Decision to proceed with the project.
- Preparation of statement of requirements.
- Decision to go out to contractors.
- Selection of tender list.
- Issue of SOR.
- Preparation of response to SOR.
- Evaluation of responses to SOR.
- Selection of shortlist for tender.
- Issue of the ITT.
- Preparation of proposal in response to ITT.

- Evaluation of responses to ITT.
- Selection of a contractor.
- Approval by senior management and release of funds.
- Agreement of a contract.

These pre-project activities may take a few weeks in the case of a small project and up to 5 years for very large systems. On average it is advisable to plan realistically for pre-project activities to take at least 6 months. Some people will try to short-circuit these steps on the false premise that they will gain time and save costs. Experience in all sectors, and for all types of software development, shows that *taking sufficient time* and carrying out an effective pre-project evaluation actually *results in a lower overall cost*. This does not imply a lower estimated cost, but it does signal a much lower probability of an overrun in timescale and cost being incurred.

From an analysis of a sample of 85 projects that overran on time and budget by at least 40%, which were the subject of either a QA or financial audit, it was concluded that:

- 8% were due to insufficient attention to the implications of using technical innovation in an operational system without a proper feasibility study;
- 20% were attributable directly to poor management of the project;
- 9% were due to the setting of unrealistic timescales for the project;
- 63% were due to unsatisfactory pre-project evaluation, tendering and estimating.

Looked at overall it is clear that 80% were due in some way to the project being set up badly. The interesting thing is that in some instances it was due to an excess of zeal and enthusiasm for techniques and technology and insufficient attention to project management and commercial considerations. However, the major cause was identified as inexperience and a genuine belief that cutting out the 'unnecessary' preliminaries and getting contractors started on the job would save money.

The other key dates that must be considered at the ITT stage are the following:

- Expected start for the project.
- Key milestones which must be co-ordinated with other projects or systems.
- Target for completion of the project.
- Warranty period after acceptance of the system.

All of these should be indicated as timescales or actual target dates since they are important in the context of costing the project, particularly if some stages in the overall schedule may be subject to change at a later date; for example, rescheduling due to a change in the development of a related system. The validity period for quotations must be realistic in the context of the overall schedule. A particularly important consideration is the realism of the project mobilisation period and the stability of the start date, particularly if delays are likely in getting final project approval from management and release of project funds. All of these matters will influence the cost profile, the cash flow profile and ultimately the achievement of the planned benefits.

9.7   Dialogue

The purpose of dialogue initially is to foster a clear understanding of the requirement and subsequently to get a clear understanding of the proposal submitted. The ITT should therefore outline how the evaluation will be done and dialogue will ensure that all relevant information is included in a way that makes evaluation as straightforward as possible. In the pre-project activities adequate time should be allowed for discussion of the ITT; in particular provision should be made for dialogue with the potential contractors. The discussion should be on a formal basis and come at three stages as follows:

1. After the issue of the ITT and when it has been digested, a meeting should be arranged to give more background to the requirement and to answer specific questions on the proposed system. This can be either individually with each prospective contractor or collectively.
2. Up to the point of the closing date for proposals allow further questions in written form (telex, telefax, letter, E-mail etc.).
3. After submission of the proposals invite each contractor to make a brief presentation on their submission. It must be made clear that no new material or variation to the proposal can be made at that stage. This is an opportunity to raise questions on the proposal and to discuss the submission with the prospective contractor.

9.8   Assessing the ITT

An ITT can only be properly costed when the technical and project requirements have been assessed in detail. Also, the commercial conditions proposed, or sometimes imposed, will have an important bearing on the cash flow profile. It is up to recipients to raise questions and clarify any matters that are likely to influence the timescale and costs. It is also important to identify and raise any areas of concern — such as calendar dates, interfacing with other software or dependence on any effort not within the control of the project manager. Waiting for other people to do things or provide facilities causes delays in the schedule and disrupts planned tasks, and this is ultimately reflected as an increase in costs. Promises to provide things 'when needed' do not constitute a contractual commitment to pay for staff time wasted in waiting for facilities, or approvals, once a project team has been mobilised.

9.9   Objective in responding

The objective in responding to an ITT is to win a business opportunity and the response will provide a basis for formal agreement between the supplier and the customer. It is important therefore that the response is as follows:

- Within the technical capability of the company.
- On commercial terms that are judged appropriate to the effort and risk involved.

The basis of costing a response may be one of the following:

1. At a premium price dictated by what the market will bear. This will be based on exclusive skill or experience or the availability of a low-cost core. It is a dangerous approach and one which cannot be sustained for long in a highly competitive market. Beware your competitors who have adopted one of the more aggressive options!
2. At cost plus normal profit margin. This is likely to be the basis of the majority of proposals as it fulfils normal trading requirements and satisfies the shareholders.
3. At or close to cost with no profit margin. This will be done for two reasons:
    (a) to gain a foothold in a market area or enhance experience in a particular technique — this is an investment situation and is of little or no value unless it forms an explicit part of a marketing plan with the full intention of recovering the investment in future business activities;
    (b) to continue working, or sustain a skill base, in a period of economic recession — this can only be done for a short period of time, on short-duration projects, and limited to certain sectors of a company's business at one time.

The costing of proposals for software projects on the basis described in point 3 above requires considerable skill and judgement. The margin for error is very small and any underestimate represents a loss. There is no room in estimating for arbitrary contingency and all that was said on this matter in Chapters 2 and 6 should be regarded as of the utmost importance.

9.10   Presentation of technical and commercial information

A shortcoming of many proposals and a source of immense frustration to those trying to evaluate proposals prepared in response to an ITT is the failure to observe the following simple principles:

- State what you propose to do.
- State how you propose to do it.
- State what will be delivered.
- State what it will cost.

But even these are not enough because they should be linked so that it is evident to the recipient that the activities of the plan cover both technical and control activities and that the cost quoted is comprehensive and includes all the items needed to accomplish the work. Assumptions about payment for third-party software, provision of development facilities, travel and other costs should be clearly stated. One good reason for using the TIC template to lay out the costs in a proposal is that it is immediately evident what has and has not been included.

9.11   Stating the basis of the costs

Unless the ITT specifically requires a contractually binding offer all tenders should be submitted 'subject to contract'.

The position on taxation and related matters is becoming much clearer in definition and much stricter in application between countries in the European Community and elsewhere. If any part of a project is being done in another country or requires staff or resources from another country then the statutory liabilities should be thoroughly investigated and the impact on relevant parts of the project taken into account.

In Chapter 6 mention was made of currency exchange rates and inflation, the latter varying not only from year to year but also from country to country. In addition any combination of the following may need to be taken into account:

1. Payments to an agent or agency for all work done in the country.
2. Corporate tax on turnover in the country even though there is only a small sales force in residence or indeed only the project team for part of a calendar or tax year.
3. Corporate tax liability for any joint business activity.
4. Personal income tax for individual members of a project team.
5. Personal social security, health or welfare charges for individual members of the project team or their dependents.
6. Value-added tax or other local taxes payable for resources or services carried out or delivered to any country.
7. Customs and excise charges on the movement of hardware between countries — including disks, tapes, etc., containing software or large quantities of manuals.

Liability for these costs, who will be responsible for payment and their inclusion or otherwise in the cost estimate should be clearly stated. As most tax and VAT levels change from time to time it is usual to exclude them and state that they are an extra at the current rate relevant in the particular country, i.e. the rate applicable at the time of incurring the tax or at the time of invoicing as appropriate.

9.12   Assessing the responses to a tender

There will always be a variation in the cost estimates submitted by a group of potential contractors. The costs will be influenced by the various factors mentioned in Section 9.9. However, it is useful to be aware of some other specific points that can influence costing and produce tenders that are unexpectedly low or high.

Low estimates signal the following:

- Misunderstanding of the requirement.
- Undefined assumptions about the provision of development facilities, third-party software, etc.
- Desperation for work.
- Small organisation with very low overheads.

High cost estimates signal the following:

- Misunderstanding of the requirement.
- Undefined assumptions about the provision of development facilities, third-party software, etc.
- Pricing themselves out of the work rather than decline the invitation.
- Large organisation with high overheads.

Costs between these extremes can suffer the same defects and it is up to the evaluator to take an objective view. Misunderstanding of the requirement is a serious matter and is the cause of a great deal of wasted effort on both sides of a tendering process. It can easily be avoided by giving proper attention to the statement of requirements, or invitation to tender, and ensuring there is full and effective dialogue as discussed in Section 9.7.

Inviting large organisations to tender for small jobs will incur some overhead. Inviting small organisations to tender for large jobs will incur some risk due to a small pool of experience and backup.

9.13   Legal liability

There will usually be a statement in the contract regarding the law of the country applicable. Statutory obligations relating to both the employment conditions of staff and the protection of computer-based data should be examined. In addition to taking account of the country in which the project is to be carried out there may be other data protection legislation relating to countries in which the system is to be used. The contractors should satisfy themselves that the work will be done within the law of the various countries concerned as the financial penalties for non-compliance could be significant.

A few companies on very few occasions fall foul of the law but with the increase in legislation on computer-related matters it is important that there is an awareness of the framework of relevant law.

10 Life cycle costing

10.1 Changing environment of software engineering

Many people consider the cost of software only in the context of the system development process. This may have been true in the past but it is certainly becoming less so now and it is not likely to be representative of the position in the future.

Software is now required to meet new and challenging demands in the operational environment, and to meet those requirements higher standards and quality assessment are being imposed with a fairly fast progression towards the time when software generally will carry some form of certification.

Much of this movement has come from the defence industry where software, together with computer hardware, is now as important as the engineering aspects of the weapon systems. In parallel there has been a growth in the dependence on IT for commercial operation within all parts of the financial sector. Tax and social security systems have, more recently, become operationally dependent on IT. Software, hardware and communications have become the backbone of the working environment in these sectors of the economy and this is spreading rapidly to other sectors.

Software is the key element in operational systems and is a vital factor that directly influences the way in which the business can function. It is now becoming fully integrated into areas such as the following:

- Day-to-day operational tasks.
- Operational scheduling.
- Management and control.
- Strategic planning.

It is becoming increasingly important that software engineering evolves in a way that meets those challenges. Software engineers have got to understand fully the business environment — how the factory, office or transport system works and how it is run so that software systems can be designed that will meet operational needs in the most cost-effective way.

Because many software systems are becoming so clearly related to operational activities and management actions it is crucial that they are designed in a way that ensures adaptability to changing needs and challenges in the business itself.

It is important that software engineering, generally, adopts design and development approaches that allow for application software to be modular and adaptable to business needs. Furthermore we need to look not just upon the initial cost of developing software, with a modest allowance for 'support' as in the past, but more realistically at the true life cycle and the related costs. Life cycle and life cycle costs in this context cover the point from initial assessment through to the final decommissioning when the software is no longer suitable for operational use.

10.2   Influences on life cycle costs

Many large organisations are now recognising that information is an important corporate resource and are moving away from fragmented databases and token gestures to 'database management' to a much higher-level approach such as the setting up of a strategic software environment (SSE) in which data management including databases will be seperated to a large extent from applications software. Many of the new generation of DBMSs will reflect this changing situation. The licensing arrangements for use of SSE-type databases will have to reflect access by many applications systems and access across widely networked hardware. It is to be expected that this will result in a change in the costing basis for operational support software which is often dominated by DBMS charges.

Much of today's software has been designed with only 'lip service' being paid to modularity. Meeting changes in the business environment is, consequently, difficult and costly to incorporate resulting in software that is as follows:

- Less robust and operationally reliable.
- Without the capacity for further development.
- Not fully meeting user needs.

In many cases even modest changes in operational demands are difficult to incorporate and in some instances the system has to be redesigned and replaced, resulting in the following:

- A reduced life cycle for the software and less return for the original investment.
- Further capital investment often without any increase in the business benefit from using the system.

Design for all systems must regard a long life cycle, and integration with other systems, as a prerequisite if the SSE concept is to be effective. In particular, modularity must be seen as essential, at the design stage, so that parts of the system can at a later time be taken out and replaced with little or no disruption to the system as a whole or to the other software to which it is interfaced.

Design of all systems should now take fully into account the immediate, or possible future, need to interface and interact with other software facilities even though they may not be specifically defined at the design stage. It is surprising how many systems are designed with so-called 'hooks', to connect with other software, that are in reality more like a mirage — the closer you get the more they fade away and do not amount to anything of practical use in terms of effective interfacing.

Attempts to interface systems retrospectively have most often been difficult technically, unsatisfactory to users and very expensive to implement.

Having put a lot of emphasis on design for integration it may seem a contradiction in terms now to discuss the design of software that has a large element of independence. However, some organisations require application software systems that can function as part of an integrated set of operational and management facilities, but at the same time the systems may need to be put together in various combinations for use at different sites, located anywhere around the world. The design of future systems, in this respect, should take account of the following:

Portability

Portability will be necessary so that systems can be set up on different manufacturers' hardware at different locations. We now have some measure of portability through software languages and DBMSs that are transportable across different hardware. Functionally this is satisfactory but there are often serious doubts about this approach, on cost grounds. The user is asked to pay for an item, such as a DBMS run-time licence, that is sold with the software. This is particularly unsatisfactory when a licence for the DBMS is already held but:

- the package may use a different release version of third-party software;
- the third-party software licensing arrangement may be different in the country of destination.

The move to portable software will be greatly enhanced by the wider use of universal operation systems, such as UNIX, so that the 'system package' which has to be considered may well be some combination of:

UNIX (type) + DBMS + Application software

A satisfactory policy must be developed regarding the costing structure of portable systems so that they will be economically as well as technically viable.

Compatibility

Compatibility will also be required so that systems can be run on different configurations of hardware, particularly in terms of size. Users with a small-volume database could use a PC whilst other users, within the same corporate environment with large databases, may be running on a mainframe computer but with totally compatible application software. Upwards and downwards compatibility may well come as a by-product of true portability but potential users will expect these facilities on an equitable charging basis.

Another factor that will influence life cycle costs will be the wider use of software modules, through component libraries. Where these have been set up and used there are indications that software development costs can be reduced by about one-third. This is only an initial benefit and may grow when the facilities expand and become established for system development. The effect on system enhancement is, as yet, unknown but it is probable that there will also be a cost reduction in this area. The net effect will be an overall reduction in software life cycle costs gained from reusable software components.

10.3   Integrity and security of software

Originating in the process control area, where the high integrity of software is crucial, there have evolved some software engineering practices that are applicable, and potentially of immense value, across all areas of software development. UK Defence Standards 00-55 (27) and 00-56 (28) set out some important software engineering practices that are aimed at the minimisation of software faults through good practices and include valuable items such as the following:

- Design standards.
- Design review.
- Certification standards.

The UK Department of Trade and Industry have also issued a Guide to Software Quality Management Systems (17) covering construction and certification. This is based on ISO 9001 (EN 29001). The other important contribution to future software engineering practice in Defence Standard 00-55 is in the area of project life cycle standards which covers not only all aspects of design and development but also relevant in-service aspects. Of particular significance are the in-service requirements relating to software modifications and the objective of ensuring that any modification does not compromise the integrity of the software.

The emergence of these much improved approaches to software design and development practice have particular relevance to software life cycle costing in the following way:

- Design effort may well be increased by the use of more rigorous methods but the subsequent development and implementation of the systems will be much easier, and so the net increase in effort and cost may be marginal. The resulting system should potentially have much higher overall integrity and require less ongoing support.
- Minimising software faults by more rigorous design and development methods will lead to a reduction in systems implementation and maintenance costs.
- By ensuring that later modifications and enhancements are to the same standard as the original design, the value of the system to users is sustained and the life cycle of the software maximised. The return on the investment in software is therefore assured — if not increased.

Well-designed and well-supported software offers higher availability for business use and more security against data corruption. As far as software security systems are concerned, they should in any case be designed to high standards and have high sustainable integrity.

Effective configuration management is a must if a system is being run at more than one location or on more than one hardware configuration. Often there may be different combinations of software modules running on each site and a configuration management plan and change control procedures are essential. In the event of system versions getting out of step, or even out of control, the effort and cost of recovery is extremely high and the potential life cycle of the system may be seriously shortened with a consequent loss of benefit and a low return on the investment in the system.

10.4   Software costs in context

In the early 1950s software costs represented a small proportion of the total costs of setting up and running a system — 10% for software development, 10% for software support and 80% for hardware purchase and support. That pattern has changed radically as shown in broad terms in Figure 10.1. We are now in a situation where software development costs are about 45% of total, software support is about equal at 45% and only 10% of the total cost is attributable to hardware. The life cycle cost of software is therefore about 90% of total system costs over the useful life of the software.

In the early days of software development, programs were firmly wedded to particular hardware and often had a short life for three reasons:

1.   The hardware was too costly to keep running over the longer term and was more frequently replaced by lower cost, more effective machines.

Figure 10.1
Software development,
software support and
hardware as percentage
of total cost

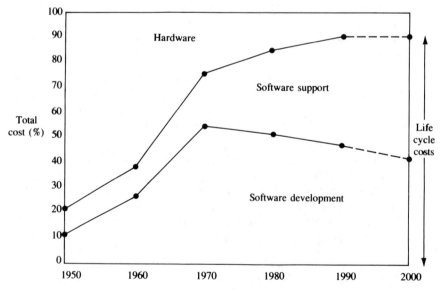

2. The software was not transferable forwards to the new hardware. Even in the limited situations where this was possible the effort and cost were high and the resulting operational systems could not easily be enhanced.
3. In most situations the software design approach did not allow for changes to the programs to meet changing business requirements.

Although in the past software costs in terms of development and support were a much lower proportion of the total cost, the life cycle of the software was correspondingly shorter and further investment was needed for replacement systems. Overall the cost of IT systems was high and the return on the investment probably not very good, although there are no figures available to support that view.

The position now is quite different with software having a much greater degree of hardware independence and in addition hardware suppliers are striving to provide onwards compatibility for a wide range of software. At the same time system design is focusing much more on modularity and flexibility so that enhancements can be incorporated to meet the changing needs of the business and this is leading towards the desirable goal of maximising the sustainable life of software systems.

Looking forward it seems likely that hardware costs will remain at about the same proportion of total operational costs — any increases in communications costs, arising from more extended use, should be balanced by a continuing decrease in the cost of processing power. This assumes that we will continue to enjoy the benefits of increased computing power for lower real costs at a similar rate as over the last decade. Software life cycle costs are likely to fall below the present 90% of total operational costs with software development falling from the present 45% to perhaps as low as 30%. This will be mainly influenced by the pattern of growth in software component libraries and the extent to which they are set up within some standards framework. The overall emphasis will be on lower maintenance and more planned and well-costed enhancements to increase the overall life cycle and the return on the investment.

The expected distribution of software costs over the life cycle is given in Table 10.1 but without taking account of any software component library influences as mentioned above. The figures for 'present' and 'future' total installed cost (TIC) have been taken from Table 4.2 and are re-presented as part of the life cycle cost (LCC). The support costs have been added and distributed over three items:

1. Operational software (continuing annual licence costs).
2. System maintenance.
3. System development and enhancement.

The underlying feature is that the initial software development costs will be less than half of the life cycle costs. The implication is that for the future 'enhancement' to software systems will not just be a few refinements that can be costed and carried out as part of the general maintenance and support. Firstly if the design and development is carried out to high standards then the amount of 'support'

Table 10.1   TIC as a proportion of software life cycle costs

Cost element	Present		Future	
	% of TIC	% of LCC	% of TIC	% of LCC
Assessment	12	6	15	6
Requirements definition	8	4	10	4
Software tools	10	5	20	8
H/W facilities for development	2	1	—	—
Design	20	9	20	8
Development	20	9	15	6
Implementation	10	4	5	2
Training	3	1	5	2
Project management and administration	5	2	5	2
Operational software	10	4	5	2
TIC	100%	45%	100%	40%
Operational software		15		5
System maintenance		10		5
System development and enhancement		20		35
Software life cycle cost (LCC)		90		90
Hardware costs		10		10
Total cost of over system life		100%		100%

should drop to a very low level. This has already occurred with many off-the-shelf packages that run perfectly well with users only making occasional reference back to the licensee. There is no reason why this principle cannot be extended across all areas of software. Where there is a need to make follow-through enhancements these should be considered specifically as aimed at the following:

- Extending the operational life of the software.
- Increasing the benefit gained from the system by developing the facilities available to users.

As such the follow-through cost of developing these facilities should be looked at as further investment that is wholly justified on each occasion and examined in the context of the life cycle of the system and an extension of the post-project cost—benefit profile.

10.5   Cost—benefit over the life cycle

The actual total installed cost (TIC) and cash flow profile at the point of completion of the project is the basis on which the success of the system development can be judged. If the actual development cost and timescale are close to the original estimate then the benefit assessed at the start of the project is likely to be attainable and at a rate close to original assessment. Major changes in costs or timescale approved in the course of the project should have been examined in the context of the return on investment and in some instances the cost–benefit expectation will have changed. There are certain circumstances that will influence whether the actual benefit from the use of the system is achieved. These include the following:

- A change in market conditions that might result in an increase or decrease in the rate of expected benefit.
- A change in operational conditions, due to corporate reorganisation, mergers, etc., leading to a change in the use of the system and a change in the rate of return.
- A failure on the part of management to ensure that the system is effective in use and that maximum corporate benefit is derived from the information-handling capabilities of the software.

The first two may be out of the direct control of line management but the third is not and is frequently the reason why systems never achieve their intended potential in operational use. It is essential, for the future, that there is a formal process of post-implementation benefit assessment (PIBA) and that the benefits are recorded as a follow-through to the project and compared with the *actual*, final, TIC cost profile. This will have value in a number of ways:

1. There will be an *actual* cost–benefit profile created that will show whether the system has achieved expectations.
2. With regular, say annual, review of the system in practice, attention will begin to focus on the system as an operational facility and enhancements will be seen as part of the process of increasing the value of the system. All too often enhancements are made without considering, or subsequently assessing, the additional return from that investment.

The *actual* TIC and *actual* cash flow profile should therefore become the basis for life cycle cost reporting and for life cycle cost–benefit assessment. This is set out in Table 10.2. The example used is for a custom system development, given earlier in Table 2.3, where the initial period of 3 years is now extended to an 8 year time base.

After 2 years of full benefit from the initial investment of £118,000 there is a further investment in enhancements to the system of £60,000 in year 5, yielding an additional benefit of £200,000 per year. Similarly in year 7 a further £50,000 is spent in enhancements with an expected additional return of £100,000 per year.

The overall cash flow profile for the life cycle of 10 years is positive after 1.5 years of operational use and continues to yield significant net benefit through the life cycle as indicated in the overall cash flow. However, it is not usual to look at ongoing cash flow in this way. Management will consider that once the system is established in operational use and yielding a regular return on the original

Table 10.2 Life cycle costs, benefits and cash flow for a custom development with enhancements

Elapsed time (years)	1	1	2	2	3	3	4	4	5	5	6	6	7	7	8	8
Half year intervals	1	2	1	2	1	2	1	2	1	2	1	2	1	2	1	2
Development cost (TIC)	18	65	35													
Operational software				2	2	2	2	2	2	2	4	4	4	4	5	5
System support				8	8	8	8	8	8	8	10	10	10	10	10	10
Development and enhancement									20	20			30	20		
Half yearly costs	18	65	35	10	10	10	10	10	30	30	14	14	44	34	15	15
Cumulative costs over life cycle (LCC)	18	83	118	128	138	148	158	168	198	228	242	256	300	334	349	364
Initial benefit				100	200	200	200	200	200	200	200	200	200	200	200	200
Additional benefit													100	100	150	150
Cumulative benefit				100	300	500	700	900	1100	1300	1500	1700	2000	2300	2650	3000
Overall cash flow	-18	-83	-118	-28	162	352	542	732	902	1072	1258	1444	1700	1966	2301	2636
Actual cash flow	-18	-63	-118	-28	-28	152	342	532	-60	36	132	-30	-50	-5	40	

investment then the system will be regarded as part of the routine operational facilities. The benefit from the use of the system will become part of the consolidated day-to-day operational return. Any further enhancements to the system will be treated as new investments that will have to be justified in their own right by corresponding benefit. This situation is reflected in the actual cash flow figures in Table 10.2 which shows each stage of enhancement investment as a negative cash flow followed by a period of payback before a further investment is made in additional facilities. The process of justifying each enhancement to the system provides a sound business basis which is satisfactory to all parts of the organisation as follows:

- Management see it as a good investment of corporate resources.
- Users see it as an effective way to get additional facilities to aid the day-to-day operational work.
- The IT department have clearly defined development targets that are in support of corporate operational needs.
- Software enhancement becomes a well-directed and effective approach to the support of a valuable corporate resource.
- A software replacement policy can be easily developed in the light of a full understanding of the past investment and benefit profile.

10.6   Life cycle costing and replacement policy

Keeping a careful watch on systems enhancement is not only important in the early and middle years of the life cycle, it is particularly important later when replacement of the software becomes necessary.

There comes a stage in the life of all software when it is no longer economic to invest further in system facilities, although continued routine maintenance is of course required.

Occasionally when this point is reached there may be some justification for minor enhancement to ensure that the system can function reasonably effectively until replacement software can be commissioned, particularly if the replacement timescale is likely to be a matter of years rather than weeks or months. In these circumstances the interim, or support, investment must be included in the overall estimates for the replacement of the system.

The other factor that could trigger some level of spending later in the life cycle of applications software is the impending withdrawal or replacement of third-party software — particularly a DBMS or graphics package that underpins the application. Some measure of re-engineering of software may be called for but the withdrawal of third-party software will often precipitate a replacement assessment being initiated.

Conditions that lead to the serious consideration of software replacement should be well understood. Neither the IT industry nor users can afford the luxury of replacing software for superficial reasons as has often happened in the past. The main things that should be examined as triggers for the replacement of software

are as follows:

High maintenance and support costs

This is likely to occur less and less with good design procedures, a well-established policy on sustained systems integrity and established procedures for systems re-engineering.

Loss of effectiveness

If this arises from increased operational demand it can, in some situations, be overcome by upgrading the hardware to give an order of magnitude increase in performance. However, the cause may be a gradual change in operational practices and conditions that cannot be anticipated or met by stepwise enhancement. In any case the design of a system can only cope with a finite amount of change before major restructuring becomes necessary. Consequently the software system may fall behind in providing the level of support needed for the operational demands. Replacement then becomes the only option if the software is to fulfil its role in that operational area.

Major enhancements

These may be dictated by any number of factors, such as market forces or changes in operational policy, and there is always a need to examine the wisdom of a major investment in a system that has been operational for some time compared with complete replacement. The decision will be dictated by a mixture of financial and technical factors that can be quantified and examined as potential benefit to be gained from each option compared with the cost of those options. One important factor in a replacement review will always be the *additional* benefit, over and above the benefits from the existing system, and that benefit may have to be significant to justify the proposed investment. It is, however, useful to have a well-documented financial profile of the existing system such as that illustrated in Table 10.2 as, in the absence of definitive information, there will always be doubts regarding the benefits being gained from the existing system.

Corporate policy

From time to time organisations see a need for change — in market share, in type of business or simply in organisational structure. With IT now inextricably interwoven with operational activities there is a corresponding requirement for a review of IT. This should not be separate or a follow-on — 'adapting the IT to meet the new challenges' — it must be carried out as an integral part of the overall review so that the future role of IT is identified and the benefits maximised. In the defence area new weapon systems, new warships and new aircraft are designed with electronics and IT as an integral part from the conceptual stage. Some areas of financial business, such as banking, are moving rapidly in this direction as are the major retail traders and some limited parts of industry. Industry in general and other business areas now need to consider how IT can be more closely integrated into the operational environment. Profitable business in any area cannot be sustained without some use of IT and whatever the nature of the IT application the aim must be to maximise the benefits to the business.

10.7   Software as a business resource

In the foregoing discussion we have in effect come through a complete circle and returned to the topic of Chapter 1 — justification. IT and software in particular have got to be put on the same footing as any other resource — plant, machinery, office buildings, factories, transport and skilled staff. There must be initial justification, there must be adaptation to change, there must be monitoring of the continued contribution to profitability and there must be a replacement policy based on and assessment of future need. All of this must be in the context of the business environment with IT supporting operational needs that are meeting market requirements.

If software engineering is to take its place amongst the established professional disciplines then there must be increased awareness and attention to the commercial aspects of this business rather than the predominance of emphasis — and euphoria — on technical advancements. It is coming slowly, but the immediate need is to focus on the value of existing systems and present a convincing case that these systems are contributing to corporate profitability. That will provide a sound platform on which to prepare the justification for replacement systems and wider use of IT based on exciting new technology.

Appendix I   Glossary of terms

The terminology used in the text of this book follows the standard and accepted meaning for software engineering terms. In the following glossary the definitions given are, where possible, taken from the IEEE Standard Glossary of Software Engineering Terminology (29).

Accomplishment cost Procedure (ACP)   A project control procedure in which costs are reported against schedule accomplishment.

Algorithmic   A method based on a finite set of well-defined rules for the solution of a problem in a finite number of steps.

Analog   A method in which a solution is derived by reasoning from a direct comparison with an existing solution.

Benefit   An advantage or profit to be gained from an activity.

Benefit profile   A method of presenting benefit or profit over a given time.

Bottom-up   Pertaining to an activity that starts with the lowest-level components of a hierarchy and proceeds through progressive higher levels.

Cash flow   The aggregation of costs and benefits, over a common time base, for a project which indicates the outflow of costs and the return of benefits.

Change control procedures   A set of defined procedures for recording changes made in systems after the design is fixed.

Compatibility   The ability of two or more systems or components of systems to perform their required functions while sharing the same hardware or software environment. The ability of two or more systems to exchange information.

Computer-aided design (CAD)   The use of computer software to aid in the design process. Systems are usually specialised for an area such as engineering.

Computer-aided manufacture (CAM)   The use of computer systems to aid in the manufacturing process. Systems are often part of an integrated production process.

Computer-aided software engineering (CASE)   The use of computers to aid in the software engineering process. May include the application of software tools to software design, code production, testing and other related activities.

Core system   A software system that is developed as standard in outline features and may be customised for any number of users.

Cost–benefit analysis   The process of comparing the costs associated with an investment with the benefits or profits. The results may be presented as a cash flow profile.

Cost driver   A parameter identified as having a significant influence on the cost of a software system.

Cost profile   A method of presenting costs over a given time.

Custom service   A software system designed to meet a specified customer's needs which are usually embodied in a system specification.

Database management system (DBMS)   A software system for the definition of a file structure and control of a collection of interrelated data stored in computerised form.

Decision support system (DSS)   Information systems that support the decision-making process in a business, particularly in the area of management control and operational control.

Delivered source instructions (DSI)   The final version of the computer instructions and data definitions delivered in a form suitable for input to a compiler or translator.

Discounted cash flow (DCF)   A method of taking account of changing value of costs and profits over time. Used to give a more realistic view of investments which are spread over more than one fiscal year.

Executive information system (EIS)   A software system designed for use by executives to provide information in a summarised form to aid planning and control.

Expert system   A software system that is focused on a specific area of application and embracing some specialist intelligence or expert knowledge.

Fourth-generation language (4GL)   A computer language designed to improve the production achieved by higher-order (third-generation) languages and often to make computer power available to non-programmers.

Function points   Program entities identifiable as facilities delivered to the user expressed as user inputs, user outputs, files and interfaces.

Hacking   Gaining unauthorised access to a computer system usually through weakness in the control and security facilities.

Information systems strategy   A corporate approach to the provision of hardware and software for the support and delivery of information across the business.

Information technology (IT)   A generic term used to describe the use of computer hardware, software and telecommunications as an integrated service.

Intangible benefit   A benefit gained from an investment that is not directly measurable.

Invitation to tender (ITT)   A document inviting a potential contractor to submit a proposal for a specific piece of work on a formal basis that may subsequently form part of a contractual agreement.

Life cycle cost (LCC)   The cost of a software system incurred over the period from initial sanction to decommissioning including cost of development, support and any enhancement after the system is commissioned. The total cost of the system throughout its useful life.

Local-area network (LAN)   An arrangement of computer and telecommunications facilities operating as a network within a limited geographic area.

Management information system (MIS)   A generic term for software systems that provide information that is used to assist managers in making decisions.

Market opportunity   An opportunity to increase the volume of existing goods sold or to introduce a new product. A market opportunity is often very time critical.

Metric   A number that is attached to an idea. A measurable indication of some quantifiable aspect of a system.

Net present value   The value of costs or benefits discounted over the period in which they are incurred to give an equivalent present value.

Off-the-shelf package   A software system available from a vendor with a defined range of user facilities and performance characteristics.

Opportunity cost   The value an investment could earn for an organisation if the funds required for a particular purpose (project) were used in another way.

Parametric values   Variables used in a formulation or model that can be assigned a value appropriate to the particular application.

Payback   The period of time required for an investment to be repaid by the cash benefit from the use of the system in which the investment was made.

Pilot system   A basic, operational, version of a system used to gain information on the functioning of the system in the user environment.

Portability   The ease with which a system or component can be transferred from one hardware or software environment to another.

Post-implementation benefit audit (PIBA)   An audit of a system after a period of operational use that is specifically focused on the effectiveness of the system in attaining the benefits necessary to provide a satisfactory return on the investment.

Post-project review   An audit carried out immediately after commissioning to record the actual cost and cost profile of the project and establish the development cost of the system. The process of analysing the project costs and generating feedback for future estimating.

Price-to-win   A costing approach in which the best estimate of costs is significantly adjusted (usually downwards) with the expressed aim of winning a contract.

Programming support environment (PSE or IPSE)   An integrated collection of software tools accessed via a single command language to provide programming support capabilities throughout the software life cycle. The environment typically includes tools for specifying design, editing, compiling, testing, and project management. Sometimes known as integrated programming support environment.

Project Office Any set of management and administrative procedures and facilities that provide the support environment for a project.

Prototyping A hardware and software development technique in which a preliminary version or part of the system is developed to permit user feedback or determine feasibility.

Quality assurance (QA) A planned and systematic pattern of all actions necessary to provide adequate confidence that an item or product conforms to established technical requirements.

Quality control (QC) A set of activities designed to evaluate the quality of developed or manufactured products.

Recovery audit A audit carried out on a project that is seriously deviating from plan and budget, with the expressed aim of identifying corrective action.

Requirements definition (specification) A document that specifies the requirements for a system or component. Typically included are functional requirements, performance requirements, interface requirements, design requirements and development standards.

Software virus A software component introduced for malicious purposes that corrupts software and files.

Source lines of code (SLOC) Computer instructions and data definitions expressed in a form suitable for input to a compiler or other translator.

Statement of requirements (SOR) A document inviting a potential contractor to put forward a solution or approach to meeting a stated requirement.

Strategic information system (SIS) Information systems that are directly relevant to the vital corporate functions and without which the organisation could not function.

Strategic software environment (SSE) An agreed standard set of software products that enable information systems to be developed, maintained and used effectively and securely.

System infrastructure The functional and physical environment in which a system is operating.

Tangible benefit A benefit gained from an investment that is evident and measurable.

Third-party software Software bought from a vendor under a licence or other form of agreement, and for which the user does not have proprietorial rights.

Top-down Pertaining to an activity that starts with the highest-level component of a hierarchy and proceeds through progressive lower levels.

Total installed cost (TIC) The aggregation of all cost items to arrive at the true cost of implementing a software system.

Total quality management (TQM) A method of removing waste by involving everyone in improving the way things are done. The techniques can be applied throughout the company and are equally useful in all departments whether production or service oriented.

Wide-area network (WAN) An arrangement of computer facilities operating over a telecommunications network covering a large geographic area, meeting corporate needs nationally or internationally.

Appendix II   The use of an analog model for cost estimating

II.1   The analog approach

It often arises, particularly in small organisations, that estimators are faced with a situation where there is little or no information available to use as a base for estimating. In such circumstances software engineers may consider that their only recourse is to undertake the estimating of effort and resource required for a new software system from scratch. This has to be done in some instances but is time consuming and for those with limited experience it is prone to error as many points of detail may be omitted. Estimating from a zero base should only be undertaken by very experienced staff and preceded by careful assessment of the requirement and supported by a prototyping exercise. The alternative approach to preparing an estimate from scratch is to select a previous, similar development and modify the known effort and cost to reflect the differences in the new development. This is the basis of the analog model approach that has been used in a wide variety of forms for estimating in many branches of engineering and has been adopted by some parts of the software industry with a moderate degree of success.

The aim in estimating is not just to establish the amount of code to be written, as this is becoming less and less relevant as a guide to software costs, but to base the estimate on an overall understanding of the requirement defined in terms of the content of the system, its structure, its linkage and interaction with other systems and the environment in which the system will function. A certain amount of caution should be exercised in choosing a base and it is necessary to look for a suitable past project in the context of the following:

- The system and its structure.
- The users of the software and the user environment.
- The system construction and the proposed schedule.
- The implementation of the system and the operational environment.

It is implicit in this that the relevant information set out above is also known for the proposed development so that a comparison can be made. The process of estimation by analogy is intended to provide a systematic, simple and effective approach to cost estimating. However, the method depends on making a comparison between the proposed software development project and one or more

Figure II.1
The analog model as
an input to the TIC
template

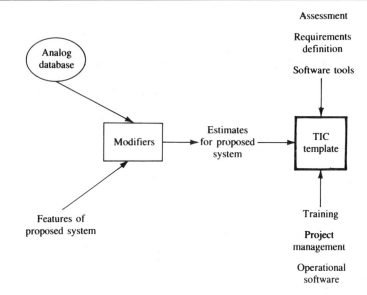

completed projects, with similar characteristics, for which the effort and costs are known and understood. It is a prerequisite to the use of the analog method therefore that an analysis of some past projects is carried out to provide a satisfactory base for estimating purposes.

The analog model can be used at macro level to give a global estimate in the early stages of development and then used in a more refined and detailed form as the design process progresses. The analog model also has the attraction that it can be used in conjunction with software prototyping and to generate input to the total installed cost (TIC) template discussed in Chapter 4. However, the analog model is not an alternative to the TIC approach — it is a mechanism for generating estimates for input to the template as shown in Figure II.1.

II.2   The analog model in macro estimating

A very simple macro-level model, in which a limited number of parameters are used, has a great deal of merit as a starting point for cost estimating. Whilst it has limitations in comparison with some other models it is useful in the following situations:

- There is no estimating methodology in place.
- There is some past project information but no detailed historical database.
- A quick, easy and reasonably accurate macro estimate is required (given the proviso of reasonable match between base and proposal).

The basis of the model process is to identify a past project that is considered to have some level of match with the proposed project and to adjust that base for

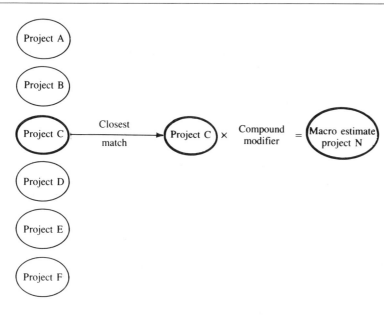

Figure II.2
Selection of base
project for use in
analog model

differences in complexity, size, skill of the software engineers and other factors which are considered likely to influence the timescale, effort and cost of the proposed project relative to the base project. This is a very basic and empirical approach to cost estimating but if it is done objectively it imposes some discipline on the estimating procedure. It is certainly preferable to more arbitrary approaches that often produce estimates without reference to any base other than the particular individual's personal experience and are inevitably contaminated with a significant degree of personal bias. The analog approach is illustrated in Figure II.2.

Initially there may be some minor problems in finding past projects with a sufficient degree of match, but the two essential requirements at this stage are the following:

1. To know the features which match and those which do not.
2. To know the quality of the data for manpower effort and costings available for the chosen base.

In the early stages of objective cost estimating, information may well be of a quality that is below expectation, but it should be accepted for what it is. Do not pretend it has qualities or features which do not exist. Even where the information available for estimating is of poor quality it may have to be used if there is nothing else. The available data should be used in an objective way and the shortcomings must be identified in the context of timescale, effort, productivity, omission of items, etc. The question of an improved base for estimating was discussed in Chapter 8 under the heading of post-project reviews. The information from current projects should be recycled as the estimating material for future work, as shown in Figure 8.1. One of the main objectives in carrying out a post-project review must be to overcome whatever are identified as the present shortcomings and improve the quality of information available for estimating future projects.

In using the analog approach for macro estimating the number of parameters, chosen to represent the differences between the base and the target, can be selected to suit the situation and to make the best use of the data available. There are obvious dangers associated with a rather random approach to comparative estimation based on 'differences' from a base and the analog approach is normally used in an orderly way where factors that are considered to constitute cost drivers are selected from a predefined check list. The validity of the analog approach does depend on the closeness of match between the proposed project and the base system and requires a very clear assessment of the 'differences' and their relevance as cost drivers. Cowderoy and Jenkins (10) emphasise the following as important if a satisfactory estimate is to be made:

- That the overall size and purpose of the previous product are roughly similar to those of the proposed new one.
- That the overall method of working in the previous project is similar to that of the new project.
- That there are either very detailed records about the work, or people available who remember it accurately.

The latter point is not particularly relevant to macro estimating as it has been assumed that, at least in the early period of use, there is little detailed data available.

The basis of comparison should centre on the broad features of the system so that similarities and differences can be clearly identified under headings that reflect these features, such as the following:

- The system and its structure:
  - · type of system and its use;
  - · system features;
  - · type and size of database;
  - · number and nature of the system interfaces.
- The users of the software and the user environment:
  - · number of users;
  - · number of terminals;
  - · number of user locations and the geographic distribution.
- The system construction and the proposed schedule:
  - · hardware configuration;
  - · third-party software;
  - · design approach and system structure;
  - · manpower loading and organisation;
  - · the skill of the design and development team;
  - · software tools to be used;
  - · proposed schedule.

- The implementation of the system and the operational environment:
    - access to target hardware;
    - system location;
    - user locations;
    - installation and testing requirements.

The objective is to use the analog model to cover all those features that relate directly to the software system itself and leave out the peripheral items that can be costed directly, such as training and the purchase of third-party software (mention of third-party software above is concerned with technical skill and use, not with the cost of licences). Focusing on the software itself ensures that there is an increased likelihood of comparing features that can be adjusted with some degree of accuracy. By implication the base system must be stripped of all peripheral cost elements before being used in the estimating process. Indeed other cost elements may not be comparable and introduce spurious errors. For example, the complexity of a system will not necessarily be any guide to the amount of effort or cost needed for training. Similarly, whilst the type of software tools to be used will have some bearing on the productivity and hence the effort and cost to produce the software, the cost of the licences for those software tools has no bearing at all on these aspects. It follows that the preparation of a database for use with the analog model should take account of these requirements and break down the actual costs from a post-project review into a format that is suitable for input into future estimating.

The use of the analog model for macro estimating is illustrated in the following example where the modifiers represent a mix of features: some that will increase and some that will decrease the base estimate. At the macro stage they should be broadly based and might include the following:

- Overall, more complex system features, assessed as about 15%.
- More menus and screens, assessed as about 10%.
- Less complex file structure in database, assessed at about 5%.
- More interfacing, assessed at about 20%.
- Use of less familiar DBMS, assessed at about 20%.
- More powerful development tools, assessed as 10%.
- Use of more experienced development team, assessed as 20%.
- More rigorous acceptance testing, assessed as 5%.

The individual degree of change from the base, such as indicated above, has to be estimated by experienced software engineers with knowledge of the base and some understanding of the new system. The differences are usually expressed as a percentage, as shown, but remember these are estimates and no one can really justify writing down 21% let alone 20.8% — the nearest 5% is realistic.

In Table II.1 the differences for the above example are expressed as modifiers.

The modification of the base cost is often done by applying a compound factor covering the modifiers for all of the parameters used. In the example given the

Table II.1 Macro estimating parameters

Modifying factor	Effect on base	Estimated	Modifier
Overall more complex system	Increase in effort	+15%	1.15
More menus and screens	Increase in effort	+10%	1.10
Less complex file structure	Reduction in effort	−5%	0.95
More interfacing required	Increase in effort	+20%	1.20
Less familiar DBMS	Increase in effort	+20%	1.20
Use of more powerful tools	Reduction in effort	−10%	0.90
Use of more experienced staff	Reduction in effort	−20%	0.80
More rigorous acceptance tests	Increase in effort	+5%	1.05

compound factor will be:

$$\text{Compound factor: } 1.15 \times 1.10 \times 0.95 \times 1.20 \times 1.20 \times 0.90$$
$$\times 0.80 \times 1.05 = 1.31$$

This represents an overall increase on the cost of the base system of 31%. In theory there is no limit to the number of modifiers that can be used but in practice there is little point in using more than about 15, and this should be kept to about 10 particularly if the percentage change in more than one exceeds 30%.

   In the preparation of the complete macro estimate it will be necessary to add the known, but substantial, elements of cost covering features that were taken out of the base system, or are additional to the base system, and which are not therefore covered by the output from the analog model. These may include items as diverse as third-party software licences needed for the proposed project, travel

Table II.2 TIC template for analog model — compound modifier

Primary cost elements	Base system	Compound modifier	Macro estimate for proposed system
Assessment	35,000		40,000
Requirements definition	40,000		50,000
Software tools	5,000		10,000
H/W facilities for development	—		—
Design			
Development	90,000	1.31	117,900
Implementation			
Training	10,000		40,000
Project management and administration	14,000		15,500
Operational software	20,000		30,000
TIC	£214,000		£303,400

costs for installation of the software at a remote location and training requirements. This can be done by the inclusion of relevant information in the TIC template. The example discussed above is set out in this format in Table II.2.

II.3 Detailed estimating

A refinement to the basic analog approach is the formulation of a checklist of modifiers against which the differences between the selected base system and the proposed system can be assessed. In this respect the simple model above then becomes parameter driven based on a much more detailed comparative assessment of differences from the base, to arrive at a closer estimated cost for the new system. If this method is to be used effectively then post-project reviews are essential to build up a database of actual effort and cost for past projects before the modifier approach can be regarded as generating dependable cost parameters. The 'difference' in system features should be quantified and applied to the relevant stages of the system development and to the relevant modules of the system.

Establishing a more detailed database on the basis mentioned above enables advantage to be taken of a further refinement to the analog model method. In the more refined form the proposed system features are matched against the features of individual modules drawn from the full range of available data. This, however, requires that past projects are examined in a consistent way and some form of decomposition is carried out. The same form of decomposition must be applied to the proposed system before the analog assessment is carried out. The estimate for the new project can then be based on the comparative assessment of modules or subsystems taken from a number of past projects. This has merit when no single past project is considered a close enough match, as a whole, with the proposed project and where parts of other projects provide a better match with the requirement — the aim of course is to draw widely on past experience and use the best information available. The process of matching decomposed project information is illustrated in Figure II.3.

The position regarding matching is even more favourable if the new development can be based directly on a previous software development. Particular examples are as follows:

- Custom system used as the basis for a package.
- Custom system used as the basis for a bespoke development.
- Core system used as the basis for a bespoke development.
- Core system used as the basis for a package.

Where modules of software can be reused in their entirety in a new system there is the added bonus that they are proven in operation. When, at some future date, the software industry and its customers realise the enormous long-term advantage of reusable software, then costs can be estimated with more certainty and software will hopefully be available at much lower cost than at present, once the initial investment in the new approach has been absorbed. However, in the interim, and this may be a decade or more, there will be continued reliance on past system

Figure II.3
Selection of base
modules for use with
analog model

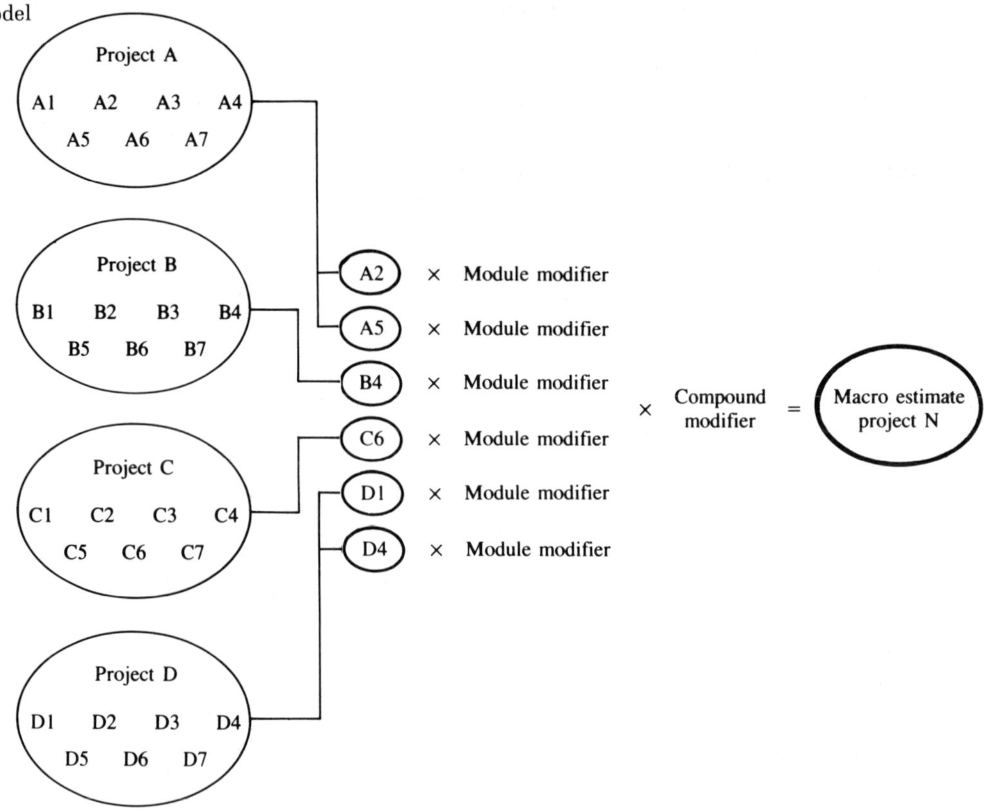

developments as the main source of data for forward estimating and we must
continue to refine the way in which that data can be used for maximum benefit.

II.4   Rules for using the analog method

There are certain rules that need to be considered in the use of the analog model
for detailed estimating as follows:

1. Do not assign a modifier to the overall system estimate if it is better applied
   to the module and of course vice versa.
2. Be very cautious about applying modifiers with large changes from the base
   system, say larger than 30% — it is better to look for a closer match or carry
   out a prototyping exercise.
3. If parts of the base are drawn from different software developments they may
   have been done at different times and the effort and costs apply to different
   years — also the skill levels may vary widely for the data from chosen modules
   and the costs cannot be modified with an overall inflationary factor.

4. Where possible apply modifiers to the resource units (man weeks, etc.) and multiply by the current unit cost, but care should also be taken to ensure the productivity rate of the resource has been checked.
5. Do not use modifiers with small percentage changes, 5% steps are all that is realistic. The only exception to this rule is for inflation which should always be the official government figure for the relevant country.
6. Where differences are substantially additive due to additional work above the base activity do not use a modifier; it is far more reliable to add an activity to the project and of course the project plan.

The analog model estimates should be developed in parallel with the project plan and the costing of the resources can be distributed over the duration of the tasks. This again endorses the remarks made in Chapter 5, and elsewhere, that a one-to-one correspondence between planning activities and estimated cost items is essential.

II.5   Modifying features

For detailed estimating as discussed above it is necessary to build up a checklist of potential cost drivers — these are factors that may be chosen in some combination to generate appropriate modifiers. These modifiers should be applicable to the separate stages of development and to the individual modules of software and not applied overall as in the macro model above.

A brief classified list of modifiers is given in Section II.6. The list of modifying factors should be built up to suit the particular needs of the organisation or the type of software developed and, where appropriate, it is particularly important to cover special needs such as high-integrity systems or detailed security facilities. The modifier checklist is not static and must be adapted to changing circumstances and needs.

II.6   Modifier checklist

The following checklist is for guidance and should be adapted and refined to meet the needs of a particular situation. However, this should not be done on a 'personal' basis as it is essential that the database created and the estimates based on that data are in an agreed corporate format and to an agreed corporate standard.

The System and its structure

- Type of system and its use.
- System features — decomposition into modules.
- Description and metric definition of each module.
- User facilities, inputs, outputs and enquiries.
- Metric definition of menus and screens.
- Type and size of database (master files and other files).

- Data structure and metric definition of data.
- Database classification and security requirements.
- Metric definition of logical internal functions (file transfers, etc.).
- Number and nature of the system interfaces.
- Metric definition of logical external functions (level and nature of interface activity).

The users of the software and the user environment

- Number of concurrent users.
- Number of enquiry-only users.
- Number of input users.
- Number of report-generating users.
- Number of terminals.
- Number of user locations and the geographic distribution.

The system construction and the proposed schedule

- Hardware configuration for development.
- Shared or exclusive access to development hardware.
- Development infrastructure proven or new.
- Target hardware configuration.
- Third-party software for development.
- Third-party software requiring modification.
- Design approach and system structure.
- Constraints on manpower loading and organisation.
- Software tools to be used.
- The skill of the design and development team.
- Training requirement for development team.
- Proposed schedule and mobilisation of team.

The implementation of the system and the operational environment

- Access to target hardware.
- Operational infrastructure functioning.
- System installation location.
- Number of user locations.
- Defined installation requirements.
- Defined test database.
- Defined arrangements for data loading.
- Defined acceptance testing.

Appendix III Preparing an estimate using the TIC template

III.1 The TIC approach

The total installed cost template approach was discussed in Chapter 4 and in the preparation of a detailed cost estimate in Chapter 6. The underlying requirement in software estimating is to be aware of the following:

1. That the cost of software is made up a number of factors such as:

    (a) effort to develop the code;
    (b) tools and facilities for development and support;
    (c) expenses involved in travel for system implementation;
    (d) effort to manage the whole process.

    These costs may arise internally in the organisation, externally from the use of contractors or from quotations for the supply of software support facilities.
2. In the estimating process account must be taken of the influence of forward inflation and exchange rates on staff rates and bought-in goods and services.
3. That estimating is an iterative process which requires a flexible base so that changes can be taken into account from whatever source they may arise, be it:

    (a) changes in software design or structure;
    (b) changes in project planning or calendar schedule;
    (c) changes in tools or facilities.

The TIC template approach is flexible and able to embrace the requirements that arise from these sources and is a fast and effective facility when set up on a spreadsheet system. In a multi-access system it is possible for several people to work simultaneously on different major elements once the timescale and general structure of the system have been defined.

III.2 Input from models

The TIC template approach is not an alternative to the use of any software estimating model. It is complementary to models and can take output from any source and add to that output elements of cost which cannot be covered by such models, such as costs arising from the purchase or use of third-party software including CASE tools. The relationship between estimating models, such as those

155

discussed in Chapter 3, and the TIC template is illustrated in Figure 4.1 and specifically for the analog model in Figure II.1.

III.3   Macro estimating

The use of the TIC template for macro estimating is illustrated below for a large and complex stock control system (see also Section 4.16). The macro estimate has been prepared using the analog model discussed in Appendix II and in this case is based on the assumption that the user requirements can be satisfied by an existing project with some customisation to meet specific operational needs. The estimate has been based on a previous project where similar customisation was undertaken. The principal variations between the target system and the base

Table III.1   Macro estimating parameters

Modifying factor	Effect on base	Estimated change from base	Modifier
Overall more complex system	Increase in effort	+20%	1.20
More menus and screens	Increase in effort	+15%	1.15
More complex file structure	Increase in effort	+20%	1.20
More interfacing required	Increase in effort	+20%	1.20
More familiar DBMS	Decrease in effort	−10%	0.90
Use of more powerful tools	Reduction in effort	−15%	0.85
Use of more experienced staff	Reduction in effort	−20%	0.80
More rigorous acceptance tests	Increase in effort	+10%	1.10

Table III.2   Macro estimate using analog model

Primary cost elements	Base system	Compound modifier	Macro estimate for proposed system
Assessment	270,000		300,000
Requirements definition	40,000		50,000
Software tools	5,000		10,000
H/W facilities for development	45,000		50,000
Design			
Development	184,000	1.34	246,000
Implementation			
Training	20,000		150,000
Project management and administration	40,000		50,000
Operational software	200,000		250,000
TIC	£804,000		£1,106,000

system are identified and quantified in Table III.1 together with the relevant modifiers for the estimate. The compound modifier is as follows:

$$\text{Compound factor: } 1.20 \times 1.15 \times 1.20 \times 1.20 \times 0.90 \times 0.85$$
$$\times 0.80 \times 1.10 = 1.34$$

This is applied to the relevant part of the system in Table III.2. The other elements of the TIC table involving staff effort have been adjusted for changes from the base and are based on preliminary quotes from external sources.

III.4 Detailed estimating using the TIC template

As in all practical situations there is often a change of approach between the macro estimate and a more detailed look at the system requirements. In the example used here detailed examination revealed that there was no package which matched the requirements and it was necessary to base the system development on a core system and undertake a major programme of customisation. This gave rise to a significant change in the overall project costs, as shown in Table 4.14, for the pre- and post-specification estimates compared with the macro estimate. The preparation of the detailed costing, using the TIC template approach, is discussed below for the pre-specification estimate.

The main steps in detailed estimating were covered in Chapter 6. Here we are concerned with applying those steps to arrive at a built-up cost. For each element the following has to be established:

- Staff effort, by class of staff, distributed over a nominal, but realistic, timescale.
- Unit rate for each class of staff.
- Direct costs broken down as regular charges (month by month) or periodic (quarterly) or once-off.
- Possible effect of inflation over the timescale of the project and any allowance that must be made for variation in currency exchange rates (usually applicable to travel and subsistence and the purchase of third-party software).

These items are entered on the appropriate cost element tables, firstly as effort and then as costs. The relevant figures are given in Tables III.3 to III.13 but in this example no account has been taken of inflation.

The preparation of estimates in this way may seem tedious to those who usually carry out what passes for cost estimating by creating forms or spreadsheets that fit the needs of the current piece of work in hand. However, the purpose of this approach is to bring order and consistency to the estimating process so that there is a sound basis and approach that can be used as part of an integrated project support environment (IPSE). It is also important to recognise that by incorporating all of the relevant factors as base information into the initial spreadsheet it is very easy to carry out changes and rework the estimate at a later time. This is important for the iterative process of estimating in the early stages but it is also of inestimable value when any changes are required at a later time.

Table III.3(a)   Assessment — effort and rates

Primary cost elements	Elapsed time from start — in quarter years										£/day
	1	2	3	4	5	6	7	8	9	10	
Justification:											
Study team	96										500
consultants	100										1,000
Technical feasibility:											
study team	48	64									500
consultants	20	60									1,000
prototyping											
Macro estimating		16									500
Cost—benefit assessment		16									500

Table III.3(b)   Assessment — costs

Primary cost elements	Elapsed time from start — in quarter years										Total
	1	2	3	4	5	6	7	8	9	10	
Justification:											
Study team	48,000										48,000
consultants	100,000										100,000
Technical feasibility:											
study team	24,000	32,000									56,000
consultants	20,000	60,000									80,000
prototyping											
Macro estimating		8,000									8,000
Cost—benefit assessment		8,000									8,000
Assessment costs	192,000	108,000									£300,000

Table III.4(a)   Requirements definition — effort and rates

Primary cost elements	Elapsed time from start — in quarter years										£/day
	1	2	3	4	5	6	7	8	9	10	
Preparation of functional specification			60	50							500
Review of funcational specification				5 2							400 1,000
Infrastructure specification			10	10							400
Preparation of statement of requirements				50	40						400
Evaluation of statement of requirements				8 5							400 1,000
Preparation of invitation to tender											
Evaluation of responses to invitation to tender											

Table III.4(b) Requirements definition — costs

Primary cost elements	\multicolumn{10}{c}{Elapsed time from start — in quarter years}	Total
	1	2	3	4	5	6	7	8	9	10	
Preparation of functional specification			30,000	25,000							55,000
Review of functional specification				2,000							2,000
				2,000							2,000
Infrastructure specification			4,000	4,000							8,000
Preperation of statement of requirements			20,000	16,000							36,000
Evaluation of statement of requirements				3,200							3,200
				5,000							5,000
Preparation of invitation to tender											
Evaluation of responses to invitation to tender											
Requirements definition costs			54,000	57,200							£111,200

Table III.5 Software tools — costs

Primary cost elements	\multicolumn{10}{c}{Elapsed time from start — in quarter years}	Total
	1	2	3	4	5	6	7	8	9	10	
Design and coding tools:											
CASE tools					16,000						16,000
languages											
development DBMS					30,000						30,000
Project management and administration											
word processing			1,000								1,000
desktop publishing											
project planning			2,000								2,000
project accounting			1,000								1,000
estimating model											
Software tools costs			4,000		46,000						£50,000

Table III.6 Hardware for development — costs

| Primary cost elements | Elapsed time from start — in quarter years | | | | | | | | | | Total |
	1	2	3	4	5	6	7	8	9	10	
Specialist hardware for development											
Specialist hardware for operation											
Additional terminals for development					6,000	6,000	6,000	6,000	6,000		30,000
Communications facilities for development					4,000	4,000	4,000	4,000	4,000		20,000
Hardware for development					10,000	10,000	10,000	10,000	10,000		£50,000

Table III.7(a) Design — effort and rates

| Primary cost elements | Elapsed time from start — in quarter years | | | | | | | | | | £/day |
	1	2	3	4	5	6	7	8	9	10	
System specification					60						400
System prototyping											
Detailed requirements specification					90						400
Architectural design					60						400
Module design and specification					80	40					350
Software design and specification					20	120					350
Specification of systems tests					60						400
Design and specification of acceptance tests						100					400
Specification of documentation					20	75					400
Specification of data transfer/ take-on					120	60					400

Table III.7(b) Design — costs

| Primary cost elements | Elapsed time from start — in quarter years | | | | | | | | | | Total |
	1	2	3	4	5	6	7	8	9	10	
System specification					24,000						24,000
System prototyping											
Detailed requirements specification					36,000						36,000
Architectural design					24,000						24,000
Module design and specification					28,000	14,000					42,000
Software design and specification					7,000	42,000					49,000
Specification of system tests					24,000						24,000
Design and specification of acceptance tests						40,000					40,000
Specification of documentation					8,000	30,000					38,000
Specification of data transfer/take-on					48,000	24,000					72,000
Design costs					199,000	150,000					£349,000

Table III.8(a)   Development — effort and rates

Primary cost elements	Elapsed time from start — in quarter years										£/day
	1	2	3	4	5	6	7	8	9	10	
Software coding and unit testing					20	240	200				350
Module testing						160	150				350
Subsystem linking and testing						250	200				300
System integration						100	300				300
System interface testing							180				300
On-line help testing							120				300
User documentation					50	60	120				350
System documentation					50	70	100				350

Table III.8(b)   Development — costs

Primary cost elements	Elapsed time from start — in quarter years										Total
	1	2	3	4	5	6	7	8	9	10	
Software coding and unit testing					7,000	84,000	70,000				161,000
Module testing						56,000	52,500				108,000
Subsystem linking and testing						75,000	60,000				135,000
System integration						30,000	90,000				120,000
System interface testing							54,000				54,000
On-line help testing							36,000				36,000
User documentation					17,500	21,000	42,000				80,500
System documentation					17,500	24,500	35,000				77,000
Development costs					42,000	290,500	439,500				£772,000

Table III.9(a)   Implementation — effort and rates

Primary cost elements	Elapsed time from start — in quarter years										£/day
	1	2	3	4	5	6	7	8	9	10	
Preparation and loading of acceptance test database					100	40 100					400 200
Functional acceptance testing								40			350
Stress testing								40			350
Installation and commissioning								10			350
Data clean-up and restructuring					300	360	400				200
Database loading								120			350
Manual data loading							300	100			200
Operational acceptance testing								20			350
Fault listing and fault rectification								10	40		350
Decommissioning of existing system									40		350

Table III.9(b)   Implementation — costs

Primary cost elements	Elapsed time from start — in quarter years										Total
	1	2	3	4	5	6	7	8	9	10	
Preparation and loading of acceptance test database					20,000	16,000 20,000					16,000 40,000
Functional acceptance testing								14,000			14,000
Stress testing								14,000			14,000
Installation and commissioning								3,500			3,500
Data clean-up and restructuring					60,000	72,000	80,000				212,000
Database loading								42,000			42,000
Manual data loading							60,000	20,000			80,000
Operating acceptance testing								7,000			7,000
Fault listing and fault rectification								3,500	14,000		17,500
Decommissioning of existing system									14,000		14,000
Implementation costs					80,000	108,000	140,000	104,000	28,000		£460,000

Table III.10(a)   Training — effort and rates

Primary cost elements	Elapsed time from start — in quarter years										£/day
	1	2	3	4	5	6	7	8	9	10	
Training of project team											
Design and loading of training database					10 20						400 200
Preparation of training programme						40	20				400
Training of operational support staff							5				400
Training of help desk							5				400
Training of users								60	60 60	60 60	400 200

Table III.10(b) Training — costs

Primary cost elements	Elapsed time from start — in quarter years										Total
	1	2	3	4	5	6	7	8	9	10	
Training of project team											
Design and loading of training database					4,000 4,000						4,000 4,000
Preparation of training programme						16,000	8,000				24,000
Training of operational support staff							2,000				2,000
Training of help desk							2,000				2,000
Training of users								24,000	24,000 21,000	24,000 21,000	72,000 42,000
Training costs					8,000	16,000	12,000	24,000	45,000	45,000	£150,000

Table III.11(a) Project management and administration — effort and rates

Primary cost elements	Elapsed time from start — in quarter years										£/day
	1	2	3	4	5	6	7	8	9	10	
Project management					60	60	60	60	60	60	500
Project administration				30	60	60	60	60	60	60	80
Administrative hardware											
Administrative stationery											
Accommodation at project site											
Accommodation at remote site											
Travel and subsistence costs	40	40	40	40		20	20	60			120
QA, QC and audit											
Cost estimating and project accounting											
Project planning and project control	2	2	2	2		2		1			100
Staff recruiting costs											

Table III.11(b) Project management and administration — costs

Primary cost elements	Elapsed time from start — in quarter years										Total
	1	2	3	4	5	6	7	8	9	10	
Project management					30,000	30,000	30,000	30,000	30,000	30,000	180,000
Project administration				2,400	4,800	4,800	4,800	4,800	4,800	4,800	31,200
Administrative hardware			500				500				1,000
Administrative stationery											
Accommodation at project site											
Accommodation at remote site											
Travel and subsistence costs	4,800	4,800	4,800	4,800		2,400	2,400	7,200			31,200
QA, QC and audit											
Cost estimating and project accounting											
Project planning and project control	200	200	200	200		200		100			1,100
Staff recruiting costs											
Project management and administration costs	5,000	5,000	5,500	7,400	34,800	37,400	37,700	42,100	34,800	34,800	£244,500

Table III.12 Operational software — costs

Primary cost elements	Elapsed time from start — in quarter years										Total
	1	2	3	4	5	6	7	8	9	10	
CAD package											
DBMS									30,000		30,000
Graphics package											
System security software							5,000			5,000	10,000
Operational environment											
Applications package					140,000			14,000			154,000
Operational software costs					140,000		5,000	14,000	30,000	5,000	£194,000

Table III.13 Total installed cost template — cost profile

Primary cost elements	Elapsed time from start — in quarter years										Total
	1	2	3	4	5	6	7	8	9	10	
Assessment	192,000	108,000									300,000
Requirements definition			54,000	57,200							111,200
Software tools		4,000			46,000						50,000
H/W facilities for development					10,000	10,000	10,000	10,000	10,000		50,000
Design					199,000	150,000					349,000
Development					42,000	290,000	439,500				772,000
Implementation					80,000	108,000	140,000	104,000	28,000		460,000
Training					8,000	16,000	12,000	24,000	45,000	45,000	150,000
Project management and administration	5,000	5,000	5,000	7,400	34,800	37,400	37,700	42,100	34,800	34,800	244,500
Operational software					140,000		5,000	14,000	30,000	5,000	194,000
TIC	197,000	117,000	59,500	64,600	559,800	611,900	644,200	194,100	147,800	84,800	£2,680,000

III.5   Overall improvement in costing of software

When setting up a system of software cost estimating it is useful to examine how it will contribute to not only the management of projects but also the overall management of the IT facilities. Once a body of consistent data has been built up the TIC records are a powerful source of information for all matters relating to IT costs. It can be used as a base for review and forward planning and in particular for addressing issues such as the following:

- Is the cost of software tools being apportioned equitably across all relevant projects?
- Is spending on project management satisfactory?
- Is macro estimating effective and improving over time?
- Is there an overall improvement in the quality of estimating?
- Are post-project reviews being carried out for all projects?
- Are the data from post-project reviews being used to improve the estimating process?
- Are project overruns, both time and money, being reduced?

There are of course many other important issues that can be looked at, and an improved measure of control introduced, once the relevant data is available.

Appendix IV How to install successful computer systems

SYSTEMBUILD — A Management Checklist (reproduced by kind permission of SD-Scicon)

The three major aspects about which any management must be concerned when it proposes to develop a new computer system are as follows:

- The system must do what is needed.
- It must be ready on time.
- You must know what it will cost.

SYSTEMBUILD is the result of thousands of man years of experience. The SYSTEMBUILD service can be used at any stage of a project. It is completely modular and is in six parts, any of which may be used individually:

1. Feasibility study.
2. Definition of requirements.
3. System design.
4. Production.
5. Implementation.
6. Support.

Using the checklist

The scope and action list of any computer project will vary with its size and requirements. Set out in the following is a summary of the tasks covered in the SYSTEMBUILD service. The checklist can be used for developments carried out within an IT department or by other suppliers of services or simply to gain an insight into what is involved in computer system development.

IV.1 Feasibility study
Set up study

1. Draw up a draft overall project plan from the initial problem statement provided by the users.
2. Take draft terms of reference and refine them so that they are agreed by all concerned.

3. Draw up a detailed project plan for this module, listing all relevant actions, all personnel to be consulted and a time schedule.
4. Draw up a quality assurance plan, defining how the project will be run, to ensure high quality.
5. Define format and contents of feasibility report to be produced.
6. Ensure that all concerned in producing the feasibility study understand the foregoing report.

Analyse existing system

7. Interview relevant personnel to gain an adequate understanding of the objectives and procedures of the existing system.
8. Examine documentation of existing system for the same purpose.
9. Document how information is passed around (data flows) the current system in outline.
10. List the perceived strengths and weaknesses of the current system.

Outline the required system

11. Use the information gathered so far to outline the requirements of the new system.
12. Create an outline description of the required system showing the data held, the inputs required and the outputs produced, and the relationship between them (data structure).

Review proposed system with user personnel

13. Circulate the outline description of the proposed system to all personnel interviewed and other interested parties.
14. Set deadline for comments and clarify any points before the deadline.
15. Document all comments received.

Investigate possible solutions in outline

16. On the basis of the foregoing, devise and propose different possible solutions, including any manual alternative.
17. Provide outline costs for each possible solution and agree outline benefits with the users.
18. Make recommendations based on this investigation.

Report on feasibility study

19. Check all actions described at the set-up stage have been performed.
20. Write feasibility report according to format and contents established at the set-up stage.

21. Present the report to the users.
22. Accept comments and revise contents of the report. Ensure that it is agreed as the basis for any possible further actions.

Conclude feasibility study

23. Have feasibility report signed and published.
24. Elaborate report recommendations into costed plans for the next stage (requirements definition).
25. Revise original overall project plan accordingly.

IV.2   Definition of requirements
Set up the requirements definition

26. Meet users to agree terms of reference.
27. Create a detailed schedule of actions for this stage of the project, including interviews with relevant user personnel.
28. Allocate staff to tasks and responsibilities.
29. Create a schedule of formal progress reviews, highlighting any milestones and task dependencies.
30. Update the quality assurance plan to be used in controlling the work done at this stage.
31. Set up change control procedures for all documents.

Define the system requirements specification

32. Refine the description of the existing system produced in the previous stage.
33. Examine in greater detail the previously listed problem areas of the existing system and examine also any attributes to be added in the new system.
34. Extend the outline description of the new system accordingly, providing a catalogue of the functions to be performed and a list of all documents and other items to be processed (data entities).
35. Agree the format and contents of the system requirements specification, the main document to be presented at the end of this stage.

Analyse the functions required

36. Gather all information needed to describe, in detail, each function in the function catalogue, including error reporting, security requirements and frequency of running.
37. Access different ways of carrying out each function.
38. Link functions and resolve any conflicts or mismatches.
39. Describe the data flow for each function and update the list of data entities produced previously.

40. Examine interfaces with other systems and ensure that there are no conflicts.
41. List all assumptions and constraints which emerge from this work.

Analyse the data required

42. Gather information necessary to refine the data structure, describing the relationship between all items of data held.
43. Expand the list of data entities accordingly.
44. Establish data volumes.

Define type of computer system required

45. Use descriptions of functions and data to infer type of computer facility required, taking into account existing and planned facilities.
46. Use run frequencies and data volumes to infer the performance characteristics needed.
47. Investigate whether available software packages could satisfy the whole or part of the requirements.
48. In conjunction with the users, define the characteristics of the man—machine interface needed.
49. Draw up a list of the key functions required, so that different solutions can be assessed.

Review draft system requirements specification

50. Gather the documentation produced so far into a draft system requirements specification.
51. Circulate and review the draft with the users.
52. Modify the draft as necessary to incorporate comments and to achieve an agreed draft.

Define the system documentation required

53. Examine existing documentation standards, if any.
54. Draw up a list of the system manuals required and describe the purpose, contents, layout and style of each.
55. Schedule, in outline, the production of manuals.

Define system testing strategy

56. Examine existing testing standards.
57. Agree a framework for testing the system, including responsibilities for providing test date and checking and documenting results.
58. Draft the formal system acceptance criteria.

Define system installation strategy

59. List all functions relevant to installing the system after acceptance, e.g. user training, data collection, system changeover, impact on staff, maintenance and support.
60. Establish how users wish each of these functions to be handled.

Produce system requirements specification

61. Produce a final draft of the system requirements specification.
62. Present it to users and incorporate final comments.

Conclude definition of requirements

63. Check all work defined in the set-ups has been carried out.
64. Review system requirements specification and the documentation, testing and installation strategies with the users, so that this stage can be signed off.
65. Place all documents under change control.
66. Produce detailed, costed plans for the next stage.
67. Revise the overall project plan to reflect latest knowledge.

IV.3 System design
Set up system design

68. Agree terms of reference for this stage.
69. Draw up schedules of actions and reviews and allocate responsibilities, as in the set-up step of previous stages.
70. Extend quality assurance plan to cover new activities.
71. Agree the format and contents of the system design specification, the major result of work in this stage.

Decide computer system

72. Use the key features required, drawn up in the previous stage, to evaluate alternative computer systems.
73. Decide the hardware, including communications equipment if relevant, and system software to be used.
74. Decide the development tools to be used in the design and construction of the new system.
75. Acquire the chosen system.
76. Schedule any training/familiarity time required.
77. Draw up an installation plan for the equipment.

Define operational features

78. Refine the previously produced description of the man–machine interface, in consultation with the users.
79. Define the desired help facilities and dialogue structures.
80. Define system management procedures such as security, backup and recovery.
81. Review and revise outlines of user and operations documentation accordingly.

Design of data

82. Apply the definitions of the previous stage to design layouts for inputs and outputs. Agree with users.
83. Develop a complete model for all data held and their relationships.
84. Produce a specification of the actual data storage, using a chosen system software (e.g., database management system).
85. Evaluate the performance characteristics resulting from this data specification to ascertain probable service levels.
86. Record any conflicts in requirements and discuss them with the users.
87. Refine specification, and requirements if necessary, until requirements are all satisfied.

Design the functions

88. From the function catalogue produced previously, develop preliminary program descriptions.
89. Incorporate security, audit and control requirements.
90. Estimate performance and capacity requirements of the most important functions. Check against requirements.
91. Resolve any conflicts between functions, data and requirements. List intractable ones for discussion with user.

Review of draft designs

92. Assemble the documentation produced in earlier steps within this stage to form a draft system design specification.
93. Circulate and present it to users, incorporate comments and resolve any outstanding conflicts in the design.
94. Issue the draft system design specification.

Start preparation of documentation

95. Using the documentation strategy developed in the previous stage, start work on the manuals defined.

96. Draft text with as much detail as is available and refine it successively as more becomes available.

Design system tests

97. Using the testing strategy produced previously, define each of the desired tests in detail.
98. Present completed testing plans to the users for their acceptance.
99. Start work on preparing test data and expected results.

Produce system design specification

100. Resolve any conflicts still outstanding and update the draft system design specification.
101. Circulate and present the system design specification and incorporate comments so that acceptance of it can be obtained.

Conclude system design

102. Have the system design specification formally signed off.
103. Revise the overall project plan. Produce detailed plan and schedule for next stage.

IV.4 Production
Set up production

104. Agree terms of reference for this stage.
105. Draw up schedules of actions and reviews and allocate responsibilities as in the set-up step of previous stage.
106. Extend and agree quality criteria for system production.
107. Agree documentation standards for the programs and data structures produced.

Produce program specifications

108. Match the preliminary program descriptions with the data structures and resolve any clashes not revealed previously.
109. Define the logic of each program.
110. Identify and isolate common routines.
111. Ensure that relevant standards are adhered to for each program.
112. Review the test plan for each program to ensure that its requirements are met.
113. Produce a complete specification for each program.

Install computer and system software

114. Ensure that any site preparation for the new computer system has been carried out.
115. Ensure that any necessary training and familiarisation has been carried out.
116. Install hardware and carry out acceptance testing.

Construct database/files

117. Using the data definitions produced previously, set up all record specifications.
118. Prepare the computer files or database, with appropriate indices and logical relationships.
119. Create the physical files for the database on the computer disk.
120. Load test data.

Code and test programs

121. Code and test the common routines identified previously.
122. Code and test other programs.
123. Link groups of programs and test them together.
124. Check that both coding and testing have been carried out according to previously defined standards.
125. As each program passes tests, make it subject to formal change control.

Test the system

126. Using the testing plan defined previously, carry out the specified tests.
127. Create and maintain an error log.
128. Collate all errors logged for individual programs, correct them and retest.
129. Retest system as a whole.
130. Ensure that all modifications are reflected in the documentation.

Review documentation

131. Ensure that all manuals have been updated to reflect the current status of the system.
132. Extract examples for training material from the results of system testing.
133. Check that the format, contents and style conform to the previously prepared specification.
134. Arrange for printing of manuals.
135. Establish procedures for updating and maintaining manuals in line with system maintenance.

Prepare training

136. Obtain agreement on the content and duration of training required for user personnel.
137. Develop a schedule for the preparation of training materials.
138. Develop a schedule for training of user personnel and allocate specific dates to participants.

Plan loading of live data

139. Examine all sources of data in current system to establish most effective means of loading it.
140. Document an agreed procedure in each case.
141. Write, test and document any conversion routines needed.
142. Prepare a schedule for the complete loading, checking and testing of all data.
143. Start data collection.

Carry out acceptance testing

144. Repeat previous testing with the tests carried out by the users.
145. Create error logs, correct and retest as previously.
146. Test all manuals and modify if necessary.
147. Obtain formal acceptance from the users.

Conclude system production

148. If system was not accepted formally, carry out agreed remedial actions, retest and obtain formal acceptance.
149. Review schedules for loading data, training and system changeover and extend them in detail for the next stage.
150. Revise overall project plan.

IV.5   Implementation
Set up implementation

151. Agree terms of reference for this stage.
152. Draw up schedule of actions and reviews and allocate responsibilities, as at the set-up step of previous stage.
153. Extend the quality assurance plan to cover this stage.
154. Agree the format and content of the final end-of-produce report, to be produced at the end of this stage.

Train the users

155. Check that all training materials have been prepared as specified.
156. Carry out training according to the schedule created previously.
157. Monitor staff performance after training to evaluate the need for additional training.

Effect system changeover

158. Continue and complete data collection.
159. Check all data.
160. Provide advice and support to users during familiarisation.
161. Start all monitoring and reporting defined in the operating procedures.
162. Initiate any minor modifications required.
163. List any problems and potential enhancements for later action.

Conclude system installation

164. Prepare a report reviewing installation of the system and present it to the users.

Project debriefing

165. Carry out a debriefing session.
166. Ensure that all problems encountered during the project and their resolution have been documented for future reference.

IV.6   Support
Hardware and system software

167. Define procedures for logging and reporting any faults.
168. Define requirements for service response time and check service organisation's hours of availability.
169. Ensure preventative maintenance is carried out.
170. Ensure that procedures for upgrades to system software are carried out and that their implications are appreciated.

Users

171. Set up procedures for requesting and agreeing changes and enhancements.
172. Set up outline plan for making changes and enhancements for coming year.
173. Specify, design, produce and implement agreed changes.
174. Maintain manuals and other documentation in line with changes made.
175. Maintain change control system.

Training

176. Discuss the need for training in new facilities, training for new operators, and appreciation training for managers and indirect users.
177. Set up plans and carry out training.

Reviews

178. review progress of the system as a whole at regular intervals.

References

1. Thresher, B. 'Building societies: Information technology into the 1990's'. International Data Corporation 1989. See also *Financial Times* 3 June 1989.
2. Small, B. 'The price of believing in a miracle'. *The Engineer*, 9 May 1991.
3. DeMarco, T. *Controlling Software Projects — Management, Measurement and Estimation*. Yourdon: New York, 1982.
4. Gilb, T. *The Principles of Software Engineering Management*. Addison Wesley: Reading, MA, 1988..
5. Cover, D.T. 'Issues affecting the reliability of software-cost estimates (trying to make chicken salad out of chicken feathers)'. In: *Annual Reliability and Maintainability Symposium 1988 Proceedings, Los Angeles, CA, 26–28 January 1988*. IEEE: New York, 1988, pp. 195–201.
6. Mohanty, S.N. 'Software cost estimation present and future'. In *Software Practice and Experience*. Wiley: New York, 1981.
7. Kemerer, C.F. 'An empirical validation of software cost estimation models'. *Communications of the ACM*, vol. 30, no. 5, May 1987, pp. 406–29.
8. Bailey, J.W. and Basili, V.R. 'A meta-model for software development resource expenditures'. In *Proceedings of 5th Int. Conf. on Software Engineering IEEE/ACM/NBS March 1981*, pp. 107–16.
9. Quinnan, R.E. 'The management of software engineering part V: Software engineering management practice'. *IBM System Journal*, vol. 19, no. 4, 1980.
10. Cowderoy, A.J.C. and Jenkins, J.O. 'New trends in cost-estimation'. In *Measurement for Software Control and Assurance*. Elsevier Applied Science Publishers: Amsterdam, 1989, pp. 63–88.
11. Boehm, B.W. *Software Engineering Economics*. Prentice-Hall: Englewood Cliffs, NJ, 1981.
12. Conte, S.D., Dunsmore, D.E. and Shen, V.Y. *Software Engineering Metrics and Models*. Benjamin/Cummings: Menlo Park, CA, 1986.
13. Albrecht, A.J. 'Measuring application development productivity'. *Guide/Share Applications Development Symposium Proceedings, Oct. 1979*, pp. 83–92.
14. Albrecht, A.J. and Gaffney, J.E. 'Software function, source lines of code, and development effort prediction: A software science validation'. *IEEE Transactions on Software Engineering*, vol. SE-9, no. 6, November 1983.
15. Behrens, C.A. 'Measuring the productivity of computer systems development activities with function points'. *IEEE Transactions on Software Engineering*, vol. SE-9, no. 6, November 1983.
16. DeMarco, T. and Lister, T. *Peopleware: Productive Projects and Teams*. Dorset House: New York, 1987.

17. 'Guide to Software Quality Management Systems: Construction and Certification Using EN29001. Issue 1.1, 30 September 1990, UK Department of Trade and Industry.

18. Wright, T. 'Information technology and organisational change'. *The Intelligent Enterprise*, vol. 1, no. 4, June 1991, pp. 7−13.

19. Westney, R. 'Getting personal: The missing link — found at last?' *Cost Engineering*, vol. 31, no. 4, April 1989, pp. 28−9.

20. Putnam, L.H. and Fitzsimmons, A. 'Estimating software costs'. *Datamation*, September, October and November 1979 (three articles).

21. Boehm, B.W., Gray, T.E. and Seewaldt, T. 'Prototyping versus specification: A multiproject experiment'. *IEEE Transactions on Software Engineering*, vol. SE-10, no. 3, May 1984.

22. Stanley, M. 'Software cost estimating'. *Journal of Parametrics*, vol. IV, no. 3, September 1984.

23. McNichols, G.R. 'Software development cost models'. In *Software Reliability: State of the art report*, ed. A. Bendell and P. Mellor. Maidenhead, Berks: Pergamon Infotech, 1986, pp. 145−63.

24. Keen, J.S. *Managing Systems Development*. Wiley: New York, 1981.

25. Baber, R.L. *Software Reflected*. North-Holland: New York, 1982.

26. Block, E.B. 'Accomplishment/cost — better project control'. *Harvard Business Review*, May−June 1971.

27. 'Procurement of safety critical software in defence equipment'. UK Defence Standard 00-55, parts 1&2, issue 1, April 1991.

28. 'Hazard analysis and safety classification of the computer and programmable electronic system elements of defence equipment'. UK Defence Standard 00-56, issue 1, April 1991.

29. 'IEEE Standard Glossary of Software Engineering Terminology'. IEEE Std 610.12-1990.

30. Lanegran, R.G. and Grasso, C.A. 'Software engineering with reusable code'. *IEEE Transactions in Software Engineering*, vol. SE-10, September 1984, pp. 458−501.

31. Matsumoto, Y. 'Management of industrial software production'. *Computer*, vol. 17, February 1984.

32. Boehm, B.W. and Papaccio, P.N. 'Understanding and controlling software costs'. *IEEE Transactions in Software Engineering*, vol. SE-14, no. 10, October 1988.

33. Low, G.C. and Jeffery, D.R. 'Function points in the estimation and evaluation of the software process'. *IEEE Transactions in Software Engineering*, vol. SE-16, no. 1, January 1990.

34. Symons, C.R. 'Function point analysis: Difficulties and improvements'. *IEEE Transactions in Software Engineering*, vol. SE-14, no. 1, January 1988.

Index